About the author

Adora Nwodo is a software engineer who develops mixed-reality products at Microsoft. She is the founder of NexaScale, a social enterprise offering new opportunities for projects and work experiences within the tech sector.

Confident Cloud

Uncover the essentials of cloud computing

Adora Nwodo

KoganPage

Publisher's note
Every possible effort has been made to ensure that the information contained in this book is accurate at the time of going to press, and the publishers and authors cannot accept responsibility for any errors or omissions, however caused. No responsibility for loss or damage occasioned to any person acting, or refraining from action, as a result of the material in this publication can be accepted by the editor, the publisher or the author.

First published in Great Britain and the United States in 2024 by Kogan Page Limited

2nd Floor, 45 Gee Street
London
EC1V 3RS
United Kingdom

8 W 38th Street, Suite 902
New York, NY 10018
USA

www.koganpage.com

Kogan Page books are printed on paper from sustainable forests.

ISBNs

Hardback   978 1 3986 1624 0
Paperback   978 1 3986 1567 0
Ebook   978 1 3986 1623 3

British Library Cataloguing-in-Publication Data

A CIP record for this book is available from the British Library.

Library of Congress Cataloging-in-Publication Data

A CIP record for this book is available from the Library of Congress.

Typeset by Integra Software Services, Pondicherry
Print production managed by Jellyfish
Printed and bound by CPI Group (UK) Ltd, Croydon, CR0 4YY

To God, the source of all my knowledge and wisdom.
This work is undertaken in humble gratitude for the
opportunity to learn and contribute to the understanding
of the subject of this book.

Contents

CONTENTS

List of figures

Preface

Welcome to your one-stop guide to the ever-growing world of cloud computing – *Confident Cloud*! This book takes the mystery out of the cloud, turning it from a confusing concept into a powerful and accessible tool. Whether you're a business owner, a student, or simply someone curious about its potential, the book will help you navigate this game-changing technology with ease.

Starting with the basics, we break down what cloud computing is all about, its evolution, and the clear advantages it offers. We explore the different service options (IaaS, PaaS, SaaS) and how they fit your needs. Deployment models, the cloud's structure, and its key parts will be explained simply, giving you a clear picture of how the cloud works.

Understanding the 'what' is just the beginning. This book recognizes that people often have concerns about the cloud, like security, getting locked into a specific provider and choosing the right one. We address these common worries head-on. We compare leading providers like AWS, Azure and GCP, so you can make informed decisions.

The book then dives into the practical uses of the cloud. We explore cloud storage, its different types and how it helps with big data and analytics. You will learn about virtual machines and containers, the workhorses of the cloud. We also cover cloud engineering and DevOps. We'll explain core principles like continuous integration and continuous deployment (CI/CD) and infrastructure as code (IaC). We also explore platform engineering and its impact on development. Even no-code tools, a new trend in cloud engineering, are covered, to broaden your knowledge.

Security – a top priority in the cloud – is carefully considered. We examine common security challenges and best practices, so you know how to protect your data. We also explore hybrid cloud models and cloud migration strategies, ensuring a smooth transition to the cloud.

This book will also help you to navigate cloud careers, with an overview of relevant jobs, certifications and potential career paths. Finally, we take a peek into the future, exploring upcoming trends like edge computing, AI integration, and the exciting possibilities of quantum computing in the cloud.

By the end, this book will have transformed your perspective on cloud computing. It won't be a scary unknown anymore, but a powerful tool you can confidently use to unlock its vast potential. So, turn the page, and let's explore the cloud together!

Acknowledgements

First of all, my deepest gratitude goes to God, my source for everything, for his grace and light in my career path and his unwavering guidance that led me to this accomplishment. This book wouldn't have been possible without the faith and inspiration that he has provided throughout this journey.

I am also grateful to the incredible team at Kogan Page. Their support throughout the writing and publishing process was invaluable.

To my family and friends, thank you for your unending love and encouragement. It means a lot to me that I constantly have you all cheering me on.

Finally, to the readers of this book, thank you for your interest in cloud computing. I hope *Confident Cloud* empowers you to navigate this transformative technology and unlock its vast potential. May this journey equip you with the knowledge and confidence to embrace the cloud.

## CHAPTER ONE

An introduction to cloud computing

Cloud computing is a revolution that completely transforms how we use technology. It gives us scalability, agility and cost-effectiveness, freeing businesses from the limitations of traditional infrastructure. This chapter introduces the concept of cloud computing, its benefits and the different models that exist.

What is cloud computing?

To properly define cloud computing, it is essential to have a clear understanding of the concept of the cloud. In technology, the cloud refers to a network of remote servers, storage systems, networking infrastructure and other types of computing services that collectively form a distributed infrastructure. These resources are interconnected and accessible over the internet, allowing users to store, process and access data and applications without the need for local hardware or physical presence.

Cloud computing is a paradigm of computing that involves the seamless delivery of on-demand cloud resources, over the internet. This approach transforms the way people and organizations interact with computers and access, utilize and manage data.

At its core, cloud computing shifts from the traditional model of owning and maintaining physical infrastructure to one where resources are created and managed remotely by cloud service providers. This eliminates the need for upfront investment in hardware and software, as well as the complexities associated with managing and maintaining physical infrastructure.

CLOUD COMPUTING AS A RESTAURANT How cloud computing works

In this example, I'm going to paint a picture of a real-world scenario that I hope you can relate to, so that you can paint the perfect picture of cloud computing. To put this in context, think about a restaurant containing different types of technological resources, where you don't need to worry about cooking or managing everything yourself. A restaurant where skilled chefs handle all the food preparations.

As you check out the menu, you'll find different options to choose from. Each option represents a specific computing resource, such as storage, processing power, virtual machines, networking infrastructure and databases. In the real world, this would be a variety of dishes available to cater to your diet preferences.

Similar to picking the right amount of food to satisfy your hunger, cloud computing allows you to adjust the resources according to your requirements. When you have a high workload, you can easily acquire additional resources to handle the tasks at hand. And when the workload decreases, you can effortlessly return the surplus resources.

The beauty of this restaurant lies in the fact that you only pay for what you actually consume. Just like enjoying a delicious meal without the hassle of buying groceries or setting up your own kitchen, cloud computing enables you to access and utilize the technological resources you need, without the burden of upfront investments or complex infrastructure management.

The convenience extends further, as this cloud restaurant is available to you wherever you have an internet connection. Whether you're in your office, at home, or even travelling, you can make use of these technological resources seamlessly. It's like having access to food without cooking, any time, anywhere, at your fingertips.

The evolution of cloud computing

The idea of renting computing services, which is at the core of cloud computing, actually originated in the 1950s. Back then, computers were really huge machines that took up entire rooms. They were very expensive and not something most people or organizations could afford. However, some forward-thinking people started exploring the idea of sharing these computing resources among multiple users.

One of these pioneers was Professor John McCarthy, a computer scientist. In 1961, he envisioned a future where computing power could be provided like a utility, similar to electricity or water. He came up with the concept of 'time-sharing' where multiple users or tasks could access a single computer at different times, taking turns using its processing power.

'Computing may someday be organized as a public utility just as the telephone system is a public utility,' Professor John McCarthy said at MIT's centenary celebration in 1961.

Time-sharing systems allowed people to rent computer time and use the resources concurrently, making computing power more accessible to a wider audience – people and organizations could basically use a computer without owning one. This laid the groundwork for the idea of sharing computing resources, which eventually led to the development of cloud computing.

Over time, technology advanced and new systems like Compatible Time-Sharing System (CTSS) and Multiplexed Information and Computing Service (Multics) were developed in the 1960s and 1970s. These systems further solidified the concept of access to computing resources.

However, it wasn't until the late 1990s and early 2000s that the term 'cloud computing' started gaining popularity. This was driven by the growth of the internet and improvements in virtualization technology.

Virtualization played a significant role in the development of cloud computing. It allowed for the creation of virtual machines, which are like computers within computers. Multiple operating systems and applications could run on a single physical server, making better use of resources and providing more flexibility. This breakthrough in virtualization technology was a crucial building block for cloud computing.

As the internet became more reliable and widespread, it became possible to deliver computing resources and services over the web. This laid the foundation for the concept of accessing computing infrastructure and storing data remotely, giving rise to cloud computing as a practical solution.

In the early 2000s, major tech companies like Amazon, Google and Microsoft recognized the potential of delivering computing resources as services over the internet. They played a crucial role in developing cloud computing platforms and services that offered scalable infrastructure, storage and applications on demand.

With the introduction of cloud service models, cloud computing became accessible to businesses and individuals of all sizes.

The market for cloud computing grew rapidly and it quickly became an essential part of modern IT infrastructures.

WHAT IS VIRTUALIZATION?

Virtualization is a technology that lets us make virtual versions of physical resources, like computers and storage. Imagine we have a big computer, but instead of using it all by ourselves, we can split it into many smaller 'virtual' computers. These virtual computers are like their own little worlds with their software and application, but they all share the same big computer.

In cloud computing, virtualization is important for optimizing the use of resources and this promotes flexibility. It allows the creation of virtual machines, which are software-based replicas of physical computers. Each virtual machine operates as a self-contained entity with its own operating system, applications and resources, but it runs on a shared physical server. This approach efficiently utilizes computing power while maintaining isolation between the different virtual machines.

Benefits of cloud computing

Cloud computing has completely changed how businesses and individuals use technology, providing numerous benefits that have revolutionized the digital world. Here are some of the advantages of cloud computing:

Cloud computing promotes scalability

Cloud computing gives businesses the amazing ability to easily adjust their computing resources based on their needs. Whether they need more storage, processing power or application resources, the cloud can quickly and smoothly handle it without requiring them to buy new servers.

In the past, businesses had to invest a lot of money in hardware and infrastructure to scale their resources. But with cloud computing, they can scale up or down without upfront costs. For example, during busy times, like holidays or big sales, they can quickly increase their resources to handle the extra demand. And when things calm down, they can scale back to save money.

This flexibility is great for all kinds of businesses. Start-ups and small businesses can grow without spending a lot of money upfront. They can try new ideas and see what works without worrying about expensive investments.

Cloud computing encourages remote collaboration

Cloud computing gives you the ability to access your applications and data from anywhere if you have an internet connection. This means you can work from home, collaborate with others and easily access your resources from various devices like laptops, tablets or smartphones. The beauty of it is that you're not limited to a specific physical location.

Imagine you can log in to your work applications and access your important files and documents from your home or office computer, phone or other devices. This flexibility allows you to work from wherever you feel most comfortable or productive.

Not only does cloud computing enable remote work, but it also fosters collaboration. You and your team members can work on the same documents and projects simultaneously, even if you're in different locations. It eradicates the need to constantly send files back and forth via email or worry about version control. Everyone can access the latest updates in real time, making teamwork more efficient and seamless.

Cloud computing ensures business continuity

Cloud computing can be a safety net for businesses. It ensures that your important data and applications don't exist in one place, like a specific office or computer. Instead, they are stored securely in the cloud and can be accessed anywhere.

Imagine there's a power outage or a problem with the computer at your office. In the past, this could bring your work to a halt and you might lose valuable time and productivity. But with cloud computing you don't have to worry about that anymore. Even if something goes wrong at your office, you can still access all your important resources from any other computer or device that has an internet connection. You can continue working seamlessly without any interruption. This ensures that your business operations keep running smoothly, even in challenging situations.

Not only does this provide peace of mind, but it also protects your business from potential losses. Whether it's a sudden power outage, a hardware failure or even a natural disaster, you can rest assured that your data and applications are safe in the cloud. You won't lose any valuable information and you can continue serving your customers and meeting deadlines without any disruptions.

Cloud computing promotes rapid deployment and innovation

Cloud computing helps businesses launch their new products or solutions to market faster than ever before. It provides developers with special tools and platforms that simplify the creation and launch applications. These tools take care of all the complications, so software developers can focus on their bright ideas and bring them to life.

With cloud computing, software developers can experiment and try out new ideas without worrying about expensive hardware or complex setup. The cloud takes care of all the behind-the-scenes elements, like storage and processing power. This means you can focus on being creative and innovative, exploring new possibilities and making your ideas a reality.

Cloud computing prioritizes security

When it comes to protecting data and infrastructure in the cloud, cloud providers take security very seriously. They make big investments in security measures to keep information safe from unauthorized access or potential threats.

On top of that, cloud providers have dedicated teams of security experts who monitor things. They use advanced monitoring systems to detect any suspicious activities or potential threats so that they can enforce data confidentiality, integrity and availability.

Cloud platforms also follow strict industry standards and regulations to enhance data protection. They have to meet certain guidelines and compliance requirements to ensure that they're doing everything right when it comes to security.

So, when using cloud services, your data is in good hands. Cloud providers do a lot to make sure that data is kept confidential and intact.

SAFEGUARDING YOUR DATA IS A SHARED RESPONSIBILITY

In cloud computing, security is a shared responsibility between you, as the user and the cloud provider. While cloud providers take extensive measures to ensure the security of your data, it's important to understand that you also have a role to play in keeping your information safe. Cloud providers implement robust security measures such as encryption techniques, access controls and vigilant monitoring to safeguard your data. However, you should still follow best practices, such as using strong passwords, implementing multi-factor authentication and regularly updating your applications and systems, to enhance the overall security of your data. By working together, you and the cloud provider can create a secure environment for your valuable information, providing you with peace of mind and the assurance that your data is in good hands.

Cloud computing offers cost efficiency

Cloud computing is arguably a smart way for organizations to save money (especially smaller organizations). With cloud computing, you only pay for what you use. It's like buying just the number of cake slices you want instead of ordering the whole cake. This helps you avoid spending too much money on resources you don't need.

The cloud is also really flexible. It can adjust to your needs. Cloud providers have what we call autoscaling, which means that it ensures you have enough resources when you need them and scales back when you don't. So, you never have to worry about paying for extra resources you're not using.

By using cloud computing, you can save a lot of money on upfront costs because you don't need to buy expensive equipment or software. It's like renting a car instead of buying one – you get to enjoy the drive without the big price tag. Plus, you don't have to worry about maintenance expenses because the cloud provider takes care of all that for you.

Regardless, it's important to note that, as businesses grow larger, their costs may also increase. For larger organizations, managing cloud costs becomes very important. Just like managing your personal budget, you need to keep an eye on your expenses and make smart decisions. Luckily, there are cloud cost management strategies that can help and these strategies will be discussed in a later chapter.

Cloud service models

Cloud computing offers different service models that are like building blocks, each serving a unique purpose for businesses. These service models provide different options with varying levels of control, flexibility and responsibilities. It's important for everyone to understand these models to choose the right one that matches their goals. The primary cloud service models include: infrastructure as a service (IaaS), platform as a service (PaaS) and software as a service (SaaS).

Infrastructure as a service

IaaS is like renting a virtual computer in the cloud. Imagine you need a computer to run your software applications, but instead of buying and setting up a physical machine you can simply rent a virtual one.

With IaaS you have control over the virtual computer's operating system, storage and networking. It's like having a blank canvas where you can install the software tools you need and configure the settings according to your requirements.

Think of it as having a personal computer that you can customize and manage remotely. You can install your preferred programming languages, frameworks and development tools. It's as if you're setting up your own virtual workspace.

The advantage of IaaS is that it saves you from the hassle of buying and maintaining hardware. The cloud provider takes care of the underlying infrastructure, such as servers and networking equipment, while you focus on developing and deploying your software.

If you need more computing power or storage, you can easily scale up your virtual machine. It's like adding more processing speed or disk space to your computer without physically upgrading any components. And if you no longer need certain resources, you can scale them down or release them, avoiding unnecessary costs.

CASE STUDY   Infrastructure as a service in real life

Introduction

Framey, a social travel application, has revolutionized the way users discover, plan and share their travel experiences. By providing detailed location information, attraction recommendations and a platform for visual storytelling, Framey aims to connect travellers and inspire their wanderlust. This case study delves into how Framey leveraged IaaS to overcome challenges, build a scalable and reliable architecture and offer seamless user experiences.

Challenges faced by Framey

1 *Enabling location tagging:* Framey recognized the need to tag photo locations accurately and provide users with additional information about sites. This posed a challenge in terms of data management and ensuring a smooth user experience.

2 *Scaling infrastructure:* With the increasing popularity of the platform, Framey required a scalable infrastructure to handle a growing user base and the demands of a visually driven application.

3 *Reliable performance:* Framey aimed to deliver high availability, fast response times and seamless interactions to maintain user engagement and satisfaction.

Adoption of IaaS

Framey opted for DigitalOcean as their IaaS provider, considering its simplicity, reliability and cost-effectiveness. The founders appreciated DigitalOcean's straightforward pricing model, which allowed them to build their infrastructure while keeping scalability in mind.

Benefits of IaaS for Framey

1 *Scalable infrastructure:* Leveraging DigitalOcean's IaaS, Framey built a flexible and scalable architecture that could accommodate the growing demands of their user base. They could handle increased traffic and ensure optimal performance during peak usage periods.

2 *Reliable performance:* By implementing Kubernetes and microservices, Framey improved their application's performance and responsiveness. Event-driven architecture allowed real-time notifications and reduced latency, enhancing the overall user experience.

3 *Simplified management:* DigitalOcean's user-friendly interface and automation capabilities streamlined infrastructure management for

Framey. They could focus on product development and innovation rather than spending time on complex infrastructure maintenance tasks.

4 *Security and monitoring:* Framey utilized cloud firewalls and monitored their infrastructure using the Prometheus and Grafana stack. This ensured the security of their data enabled them to proactively identify and address any performance bottlenecks.

Conclusion

Through their adoption of IaaS, specifically DigitalOcean, Framey successfully overcame challenges related to location tagging, scaling the infrastructure and ensuring reliable performance. By building a modern, event-driven microservice architecture, Framey created a robust platform that offers a seamless user experience. The combination of Kubernetes, DigitalOcean Spaces, RedPanda and other technologies allowed Framey to handle significant traffic and deliver personalized notifications to users. With IaaS empowering its infrastructure, Framey continues to inspire and connect travellers, providing them with a platform to share their visual travel experiences and plan their next adventures.

Platform as a service

PaaS is like having a ready-to-use development environment in the cloud. It's as if you're given a fully equipped workspace with all the tools and resources you need to build and deploy your applications. With PaaS, you don't have to worry about setting up and managing the underlying infrastructure or the operating system. Instead, you can focus solely on writing your code and developing your applications.

Think of it as a platform where you can develop, test and deploy your software without the need to handle the complexities of infrastructure management. It's like having a pre-built environment that provides the necessary resources, such as servers, databases and middleware, for your applications to run.

Using a PaaS, you can easily access a range of development tools, programming languages and frameworks. This gives you a toolbox with all the necessary software components readily available and it allows you to streamline your development process and speed up application deployment.

PaaS also provides features for scalability and automatic resource management. It means that as your application's demand increases, the platform can automatically allocate additional resources to handle the load; this ensures optimal performance.

Another advantage of PaaS is that it often offers built-in services and integrations that simplify common development tasks. For example, you might have access to databases, messaging systems, authentication services and other components that are seamlessly integrated into the platform. This reduces the time and effort required to develop and connect these services on your own.

An example of PaaS is Netlify, a cloud-based platform that streamlines the deployment, management and scaling of Web applications. With Netlify, developers can concentrate on coding and building their applications, while the platform takes care of infrastructure management. Netlify simplifies the entire process, allowing developers to focus on their core tasks without the need to worry about server setup or configuration.

There are several other popular PaaS offerings available in addition to Netlify. These include Heroku, AWS Elastic Beanstalk, Google App Engine, Microsoft Azure App Service, IBM Cloud Foundry, Oracle Cloud Platform, Salesforce App Cloud, Mendix, Red Hat OpenShift, SAP Cloud Platform, Cloud Foundry, DigitalOcean App Platform and more.

CASE STUDY   Platform as a service in real life

Let me share the story of NexaScale, an organization I created, where individuals come together to build and grow their tech careers. As part of our programme, a group of enthusiastic mentees aimed to develop a Web dashboard for their project. To simplify the development process, streamline deployments and provide scalable hosting options, we sought a solution that would meet our requirements.

After thorough evaluation, we decided to leverage Netlify as our trusted PaaS solution. With Netlify by our side, our mentees started building a remarkable Web dashboard. Here's how Netlify supported our goals:

1 *Simplified development workflow:* Netlify seamlessly integrated with our GitHub repository, enabling us to establish a smooth and efficient development workflow. This integration automated crucial tasks such as building and deploying our Web dashboard. As a result, our mentees could focus their energy on writing code and collaborating effectively.

2 *Instant deployments:* Netlify's deployment capabilities proved invaluable to our team. By connecting our repository to Netlify, we could trigger automatic deployments with a simple push of code. The platform handled the entire deployment process, eliminating the need for manual configurations. This agility allowed us to iterate quickly and receive immediate feedback.

3 *Reliable hosting:* Netlify provided us with reliable and scalable hosting options for our Web dashboard. We were able to handle increased traffic and scale seamlessly without worrying about infrastructure management.

As an organization committed to fostering growth and collaboration, NexaScale successfully leveraged Netlify as the PaaS solution for our mentees' Web dashboard project. With Netlify's powerful features, our team experienced a simplified development workflow, streamlined deployments and scalable hosting capabilities. By reducing the complexity of infrastructure management, Netlify empowered our mentees to focus on building an exceptional Web dashboard.

Software as a service

SaaS is a cloud computing model where software applications are delivered over the internet. Instead of installing and running software on individual computers or servers, users can access and use the software through a Web browser or dedicated application.

Think of SaaS as renting software rather than buying it. You don't need to purchase or install software on your own devices; instead, you can access it directly from the internet. The software provider takes care of all the technical aspects, such as infrastructure, updates and security, allowing you to focus on using the software and achieving your goals.

SaaS provides flexibility and accessibility, as you can access the software from any device with an internet connection. This enables remote work, collaboration and the ability to use the software on different platforms.

SaaS also follows a subscription-based pricing model, where you pay a recurring fee based on your usage or the number of users. This eliminates the need for upfront investments in software licences and infrastructure, making it cost-effective for businesses.

With SaaS, the cloud providers handle software updates, security patches and system maintenance, ensuring that you always have access to the latest features and a secure environment.

Common examples of SaaS applications include customer relationship management (CRM) software like Salesforce, collaboration tools like Google Workspace and Microsoft Office 365 and project management platforms like Asana and Trello. These applications are accessible through Web browsers or dedicated mobile apps, allowing users to access and use them from anywhere, any time.

CASE STUDY Software as a service in real life

This is going to be another NexaScale example. NexaScale is a non-profit tech community dedicated to helping individuals start and scale their tech careers by connecting them to opportunities to build impactful products. When planning the launch, we identified the need for efficient communication and collaboration. NexaScale sought a solution that would enable seamless interaction among its community members and facilitate effective management of their initiatives.

To address this challenge, NexaScale started using Slack, a popular SaaS platform. Slack provided NexaScale with a robust and user-friendly communication tool that enabled real-time collaboration and streamlined interactions within the community. By leveraging Slack's features and functionality, NexaScale successfully managed over 10,000 members across various projects and initiatives.

With Slack, NexaScale created dedicated channels for different interest groups, such as backend development, data science and product design, allowing members to connect with like-minded individuals and share knowledge and resources. The platform's chat capabilities fostered instant communication, enabling members to ask questions, seek advice and receive timely responses from experts within the community.

Slack's file sharing feature proved invaluable for NexaScale, as it allowed members to seamlessly exchange code snippets, documents and relevant resources. This facilitated collaboration on projects, enabling individuals to work together on impactful initiatives and share their progress with the wider community.

The ease of use and intuitive interface of Slack made it accessible to individuals with varying levels of technical expertise, allowing them to participate actively in discussions and contribute to the community's growth. The mobile app version of Slack ensured that members could stay connected and engaged, even when they were on the go.

By leveraging Slack as their SaaS communication and collaboration platform, NexaScale witnessed significant community engagement, knowledge sharing and project management. The platform's versatility, scalability and powerful features played a vital role in connecting thousands of individuals, helping them advance their tech careers and collectively build impactful products.

Thanks to Slack, NexaScale continues to empower aspiring tech professionals and provide them with the resources and opportunities they need to succeed in the industry.

Other cloud service models

Beyond IaaS, PaaS and SaaS, there are also some secondary cloud service models.

Function as a service

Function as a service (FaaS) is a cloud service model that lets developers run their code in the cloud without worrying about servers. Instead of building and managing servers, you write small pieces of code called functions. These functions get triggered when certain events occur, like when someone makes a request to your website or when new data comes in. The cloud service provider handles all the behind-the-scenes actions, like allocating resources and scaling up or down to handle the workload. Popular FaaS providers include AWS Lambda, Microsoft Azure Functions, Cloudflare Workers and Google Cloud Functions.

Database as a service

Database as a service (DBaaS) is a cloud service that gives you a ready-to-use database system without the hassle of setting up and managing the technical stuff, so you can focus on using the database to store and organize your data.

With DBaaS, you don't have to worry about setting up servers, installing software or dealing with complex configurations. The cloud service provider handles all that for you, making it super easy to get started with your database. You can access the database through an interface or special tools and start storing and retrieving your data. Examples of DBaaS providers include Amazon RDS, Azure SQL Database, Google Cloud SQL and HarperDB Cloud.

Machine learning as a service

Machine learning as a service (MLaaS) is a cloud service that makes it easy for developers and data scientists to use the power of machine learning without having to be experts in the technical details. With MLaaS, you get access to a range of tools, application programming interfaces (APIs) and pre-trained models that you can use to create, deploy and run your own machine learning applications. You don't need to worry about setting up complex infrastructure or understanding the nitty-gritty of machine learning algorithms. The cloud service provider takes care of all that for you.

Imagine you have an idea for an application that can predict customer behaviour or analyse images, but you don't know where to start with machine learning. You can use the tools and APIs provided by the service to build your application, leveraging the power of machine learning behind the scenes. Examples of MLaaS providers are Azure Machine Learning, Amazon SageMaker and Google AI Platform.

Disaster recovery as a service

Disaster recovery as a service (DRaaS) is a cloud service that helps organizations protect their important data and applications in case of unexpected events or disasters. It's like having a safety net for your valuable information.

With DRaaS, you can securely store copies of your critical systems and data in the cloud. This means that if something goes wrong, like a power outage, hardware failure or natural disaster, you can quickly recover and get back up and running without losing any important information.

DRaaS providers offer automated processes to make the backup, failover and recovery steps smooth and hassle-free. They handle the technical side of things, so you don't have to worry about setting up complex systems or managing the backup process yourself. Microsoft Azure Site Recovery, Zerto Virtual Replication and Zetta Backup and Recovery are examples of DRaaS providers.

Cloud deployment models

Cloud deployment models refer to different ways in which cloud computing resources are set up and used. These deployment models offer different levels of control, security and management options, allowing everyone to choose the most suitable approach based on their specific use case.

In this section, we will explore the four primary cloud deployment models: public cloud, private cloud, hybrid cloud and multicloud.

Public cloud

In a public cloud, the cloud resources (like servers, storage and networks) are owned and managed by a company that isn't you. It's like renting a part of a big cloud playground where lots of people can play. You and other organizations share the same resources, but you have your own designated space.

One important concept in a public cloud is multitenancy. Multitenancy means that multiple users or organizations, called tenants, can securely share the same cloud infrastructure while keeping their data and applications separate and isolated from each other. In a real-world context, it's like having individual lockers in a shared gym where each person can only access their own locker and not others'. The great thing about multitenancy is that it allows the cloud provider to efficiently utilize resources by serving multiple tenants on the same infrastructure. It helps reduce costs and promotes resource optimization.

Using a public cloud with multitenancy has several advantages. First, it provides economies of scale because the costs are shared among many tenants, making it more affordable for each individual user. Second, it offers high scalability and flexibility since the cloud provider can easily allocate and reallocate resources based on the needs of different tenants.

Some well-known public cloud providers with robust multitenancy features are Amazon Web Services (AWS), Microsoft Azure and Google Cloud Platform (GCP).

Private cloud

In a private cloud deployment, the cloud resources, such as servers, storage and networks, are dedicated to a single organization or user. With a private cloud, you have complete control over the infrastructure. You can customize and configure everything according to your organization's requirements, just like building your own personalized cloud space.

One of the key benefits of a private cloud is enhanced security. Since you have exclusive access to the resources, you have greater control over your data and can implement robust security measures to protect sensitive information. There is also increased privacy with the private cloud. Because you're not sharing the infrastructure with others, you have full isolation and privacy for your data and applications.

In terms of scalability, a private cloud offers more control and flexibility than other deployment models. You can easily scale up or down based on your organization's needs.

Creating and maintaining a private cloud requires more upfront investment and ongoing management compared to other deployment models. However, it provides organizations with greater control, security and privacy over their cloud infrastructure.

Hybrid cloud

Imagine you have your own private room where you keep your personal belongings and there's also a community hub where people gather, share resources and connect with each other. Now, what if you could link these two spaces together? That's what a hybrid cloud is all about.

In a hybrid cloud deployment, you can combine the benefits of a private cloud and a public cloud. It's like having your own private room for storing important files, photos or sensitive information and also being part of a vibrant community hub (or room) where you can interact with others, access a variety of services and share ideas.

In your private cloud, your room represents a secure and dedicated space where you have full control over your data and applications. On the other hand, the public cloud is like a community hub or a popular social network where many people come together to share resources and engage with various services. It's a vibrant and dynamic environment that offers scalability, a wide range of tools and the ability to collaborate with others.

What makes the hybrid cloud special is that it connects these two environments, allowing you to seamlessly move and share information between your private room and the community hub. It's like having a secure pathway that enables you to access and leverage the resources and services available in the community while still maintaining the privacy and control of your personal room.

The hybrid cloud provides you with the flexibility to choose where to store and run your applications and data based on your specific needs. You can keep sensitive information in your private cloud while taking advantage of the public cloud's extensive offerings and scalability.

Multicloud

Imagine you're a business owner looking to leverage the cloud to enhance your operations. Instead of relying on a single cloud service provider, you decide to adopt a multicloud approach. Multicloud means using multiple cloud service providers, such as AWS and Microsoft Azure, to meet your organization's specific needs.

Think of it like having two reliable vendors for different aspects of your business. For example, you might choose AWS for their robust storage capabilities and their ability to handle large amounts of data securely. At the same time, you opt for Microsoft Azure to leverage their advanced analytics tools, which can provide valuable insights from your business data.

By adopting a multicloud strategy, you can tap into the unique strengths and offerings of each provider. It's like having the best of both worlds. AWS and Azure bring their own set of services, features and infrastructure to the table. You can choose the services that align with your business requirements, whether it's storage, computing power, machine learning capabilities or database solutions.

Multicloud also provides benefits such as increased flexibility, reduced vendor lock-in and enhanced resilience. Just as diversifying your vendors reduces the risk of relying solely on one vendor, using multiple cloud providers allows you to distribute your workloads and data across different platforms. This can help mitigate the impact of any potential service disruptions and give you more control over your cloud environment.

However, managing a multicloud setup requires careful planning and coordination. You'll need to ensure compatibility between the different providers and implement proper integration strategies.

REVIEW

In this chapter, we explored the concept of cloud computing and its evolution, benefits, service models and deployment options. This foundational knowledge provides you with the tools to understand and explore the world of cloud computing further. With insights into its origins and advantages, as well as comprehension of different service and deployment approaches, you're well-prepared to dive deeper into advanced topics and make informed decisions about adopting and optimizing cloud technologies.

This chapter lays the groundwork for your journey into cloud computing. There's a lot more you could learn as this book unfolds and I am excited to take you through this journey.

GLOSSARY

CLOUD: Refers to the network of remote servers, storage systems and other computing services that create a distributed infrastructure. These resources are accessible online, allowing users to use them without needing physical presence.

CLOUD COMPUTING: A computing concept where remote servers, storage systems and networking resources work together as a distributed infrastructure. Users can access, process and store data and applications over the internet without needing local hardware.

DISTRIBUTED INFRASTRUCTURE: A setup where different computing resources are connected and work together, even though they are not in the same physical location.

ON DEMAND: Resources that can be used whenever needed, without requiring them to be available all the time.

REMOTE SERVERS: Computers that are located far away but can be used to store data and run programs over the internet.

## CHAPTER TWO

Cloud computing architecture

Cloud computing architecture is like the strong foundation that powers everything we do in the cloud. It's all about how cloud-based systems are designed and structured, helping companies use the cloud's amazing abilities to scale up, adapt and save money. This chapter introduces the fundamental concepts and components of cloud computing architecture, providing you with a solid understanding of how cloud systems are built and how they can revolutionize the way we work and innovate.

Components of cloud computing

Cloud architecture components encompass various elements that form the foundation of cloud-based systems. Understanding these components is crucial for designing, implementing and managing cloud-based solutions effectively. Let's delve deeper into each of these components:

The frontend platform

The frontend platform in cloud architecture is like the friendly face of a cloud-based system. It acts as a bridge between users and cloud services, making it easy for them to interact and get things done. The frontend platform can take different forms, like a visual interface with buttons and menus or a text-based interface where users type commands.

The main goal of the frontend platform is to give users a smooth experience. It ensures that using the cloud service is simple and accessible, no matter how much technical knowledge users have. It does this by providing helpful features.

Access control is another important job of the frontend platform. It lets administrators decide which users can access which parts of the cloud system. This helps keep everything organized and prevents unauthorized activities.

The frontend platform also makes it easy for users to set up and manage their resources in the cloud. With just a few clicks or commands, users can create virtual machines, storage space, databases and other resources. The frontend platform provides a user-friendly way to configure these resources, so users can choose the amount of computing power or storage space they need.

The backend platform

The backend platform serves as a solid foundation for cloud-based systems, where important tasks occur behind the scenes to handle data and application processing, storage and management. It comprises various components, including servers, storage systems, databases and middleware, which collaborate to provide essential computing capabilities.

Resource allocation is a crucial responsibility of the backend platform. It determines how computing power, storage space and other resources are distributed among users and applications, ensuring that each user receives the appropriate amount of resources they require.

Effective workload management is another key function of the backend platform. It oversees the smooth and efficient execution of tasks and processes in the cloud system. Prioritizing tasks, assigning resources and monitoring progress are some of the ways the backend platform optimizes performance and ensures timely completion.

Data processing is a fundamental task performed by the backend platform. It handles data storage, retrieval and manipulation within the cloud system, whether it involves storing large datasets, retrieving specific information or performing complex calculations. The backend platform ensures secure storage and easy accessibility of data when needed.

Scalability is a crucial feature provided by the backend platform, enabling the cloud system to handle varying workloads and accommodate increasing demands. Scaling up involves adding more servers or storage capacity to meet resource requirements during peak usage, while scaling down optimizes resource utilization and reduces costs during periods of low demand.

The backend platform plays a critical role in efficiently utilizing resources and ensuring optimal performance in cloud architectures. It manages resource allocation, workload, data processing and scalability, forming the backbone of a reliable and high-performing cloud system.

The backend components of cloud architecture encompass computing resources, storage, security mechanisms and management, among others. Here is a breakdown of the main backend components:

- *Application:* This refers to the backend software or application accessed by clients from the frontend to coordinate and fulfil their requests and requirements.
- *Service:* The service acts as the core of cloud architecture, overseeing all tasks running on the cloud computing system. It manages resource access, including storage, application development environments and Web applications.

- *Runtime cloud:* The runtime cloud provides the environment for running services, functioning as an operating system that handles task execution and management. Virtualization technology creates hypervisors representing apps, servers, storage and networking services.
- *Storage:* Backend storage stores the data required for operating applications. Cloud service providers offer flexible and scalable storage services designed to manage vast amounts of data in the cloud. Storage options include hard drives, solid-state drives, or persistent disks in server bays.
- *Infrastructure:* Infrastructure encompasses the essential hardware components powering cloud services, such as central processing units (CPUs), graphics processing units (GPUs), network devices and other necessary hardware. It also includes the software required for running and managing the infrastructure. Cloud architecture, however, refers to the plan for organizing cloud resources and infrastructure.
- *Management:* Real-time resource management is vital in cloud service models to meet user requirements. Management software, also known as middleware, facilitates communication between backend and frontend components of cloud architecture. It allocates resources, monitors usage, integrates data, deploys applications and ensures disaster recovery.
- *Security:* Implementing cloud security measures is crucial to safeguard data, applications and platforms as cloud computing adoption grows. Effective data and network security planning and design provide visibility, prevent data loss and downtime and ensure redundancy. Measures may include regular backups, debugging and virtual firewalls.

Cloud-based delivery model

The cloud-based delivery model refers to the approach through which cloud services are delivered to users. This model consists of various service types, like SaaS, PaaS and IaaS, covered in the previous chapter. SaaS allows users to use software applications online without installing them on their own devices. PaaS gives developers a platform to create, deploy and handle applications without having to worry about the underlying infrastructure. IaaS offers virtual computing resources, such as servers, storage and networking, which users can use and manage as needed.

Network

The network component helps different parts of the cloud system communicate and share data. With internet connectivity, the network component ensures that users can securely and reliably connect to cloud services over the internet. It sets up the necessary pathways and rules for sending and receiving data. This lets users access their cloud resources like applications and data storage from anywhere with an internet connection.

Intercloud connections allow different cloud service providers or regions to talk to each other and share data. It's useful when organizations want to use multiple cloud platforms or services and need to combine their resources and data. For example, if a company has some data in one cloud and some in another, the network component helps them work together.

Keeping data secure during transmission is an important job of the network component. It uses techniques like encryption and secure communication channels to protect sensitive information while it travels across the network. This ensures unauthorized people can't access or read the data, which keeps cloud-based systems safe.

Another important job of the network component is scalability. Cloud networks are designed to handle different amounts of work and cope with more traffic when needed. They can easily add or remove network devices like routers and switches to handle the extra demand. This helps the network keep up with the changing needs of cloud computing.

Efficient routing is also a big part of the network component. It uses smart rules and protocols to send data between different parts of the cloud system. This ensures the data takes the fastest and most efficient path. It reduces delays, speeds up response times and makes the network work better overall so that when people use cloud services they get a smooth and fast experience.

CLOUD ARCHITECTURE LAYERS

Think of cloud architecture as a building made up of different layers that work together. Each layer has a specific job and contributes to how the cloud system functions. Here are the basic layers of cloud architecture:

- HARDWARE: The bottom layer is where you find the physical components that make the cloud work. This includes things like servers, storage devices and networking equipment. These pieces of hardware allow the cloud services to run smoothly.

- VIRTUALIZATION: The layer above the hardware is like a translator. It creates virtual versions of the physical resources, so multiple applications and users can share them without any problems. This helps make the most of the resources available and improves the performance of the cloud system.

- APPLICATION AND SERVICE: This layer is where all the cloud services and applications are located. It acts as a connection between the user interface and the underlying infrastructure. When users make requests, this layer handles them and ensures everything runs smoothly. It provides different services depending on the cloud model being used, like SaaS, PaaS or IaaS. These services can include resource allocation, application development tools and web-based applications.

Virtualization in cloud computing

Virtualization is the process of creating virtual versions or representations of physical computer resources, like servers and storage devices. It allows multiple virtual environments to run on a single physical infrastructure. By separating the software from the hardware, virtualization offers more flexibility and efficiency in managing computer resources. It simplifies the way we use computers by creating virtual machines or containers that can be easily deployed and managed. Virtualization helps in saving costs, improving performance and making the most out of our computer systems in cloud computing.

VIRTUAL MACHINES VS CONTAINERS

Virtualization in cloud computing is commonly achieved through two primary forms: virtual machines and containers. These two approaches have distinct characteristics and use cases that serve specific purposes. Let's look at each of them:

- Virtual machines are simulated versions of complete computer systems. They imitate both the hardware and software functionalities of a physical computer within a virtual setting. Each virtual machine operates independently and has the ability to run its own operating system and applications.

- Containers are compact and movable software packages that bundle applications together with their dependencies and configuration files. They utilize container engines like Docker or Kubernetes to create isolated execution environments, sharing the underlying operating system kernel.

Benefits of virtualization

Virtualization in cloud computing offers a wide range of benefits that revolutionize the way people or businesses utilize and manage their IT resources. Some of them include:

- *Efficient resource utilization:* Virtualization helps make the most of hardware by running multiple virtual machines or containers on a single physical server. This saves money by reducing the need for extra hardware and using less energy.

- *Enhanced security and isolation:* Virtualization keeps virtual machines or containers separate, which enhances security in cloud environments. Each one operates independently, protecting important resources and data from unauthorized access. If there's a problem with one, it doesn't affect the others, which makes systems more stable.
- *Sustainability:* Virtualization contributes to environmental sustainability by reducing the number of physical servers required, thereby decreasing power consumption and carbon footprint. It aligns with green IT initiatives, promoting energy-efficient practices and responsible resource usage.

The different kinds of cloud infrastructure

As highlighted in the section that described the components of cloud computing, cloud infrastructure is the foundation and underlying framework that supports the delivery of cloud computing services. It is made of a wide range of physical and virtual resources, including data centres, servers, storage systems, networking infrastructure and more. Cloud infrastructure provides the necessary computing power, storage capacity and network connectivity to enable users to access and utilize cloud services. Some types of cloud infrastructure are highlighted below:

- *Servers:* Servers are the main computers in cloud infrastructure. They carry out different tasks, such as processing data, running applications and storing information. Cloud service providers have many servers in their data centres to handle the needs of their users. They use virtualization to make one physical server work like multiple virtual machines or containers, using resources well and being efficient.

- *Storage systems:* Cloud storage systems let you store and get back data in the cloud. They have big storage devices like hard disk drives or solid-state drives that connect to the cloud infrastructure. These storage systems can hold a lot of data, have ways to keep data safe and make sure it's available when needed. Users can access and control their data from anywhere using cloud-based storage services.
- *Networking infrastructure:* Networking infrastructure helps different parts of the cloud infrastructure and users talk to each other and share data. It includes routers, switches, firewalls and other devices that make connections and keep data safe. The network in the cloud is built to handle lots of data moving around quickly, have low delays and connect different cloud resources smoothly.
- *Virtualization technology:* Virtualization is an important part of cloud infrastructure because it helps make the best use of computing resources. It lets you create virtual machines and containers that can work on their own, even if they share the same physical server. This sharing saves money, uses resources well and makes the cloud infrastructure more flexible and scalable.
- *Load balancers:* Load balancers ensure that network traffic is spread out evenly across multiple servers. They help use resources efficiently and prevent any server from getting overloaded. Load balancers are important for ensuring cloud services work well and are always available.
- *Rate limiters:* A rate limiter limits the number of times a user (or client) can send network traffic to a server in a specified period of time. Rate limiters can prevent malicious activities like DDoS attacks. They also reduce the strain on the servers.

REVIEW

In this chapter, we explored cloud computing architecture and its components. This is useful for navigating today's digital world where technology plays a big role. Understanding how things like servers, networks, storage and services work together helps you make sense of how the internet and apps function.

GLOSSARY

ACCESS CONTROL: A system that lets administrators manage user permissions, ensuring authorized access to different parts of the cloud system while preventing unauthorized activities.

CLOUD-BASED DELIVERY MODEL: A method of offering cloud services, including SaaS, PaaS and IaaS. SaaS lets users access software online, PaaS aids app development without managing infrastructure and IaaS provides virtual resources like servers.

DATA PROCESSING: Handling data storage, retrieval and manipulation within the cloud, maintaining secure storage and accessibility.

INTERCLOUD CONNECTIONS: Links cloud providers or regions to share data, useful for multicloud scenarios. Enables resource and data combination, enhancing collaboration across cloud services.

RESOURCE ALLOCATION: The distribution of computing power and storage space among users and applications to ensure optimal resource utilization and performance.

RESOURCE MANAGEMENT: The process of allocating and configuring computing resources in the cloud, allowing users to create and manage virtual machines, storage, databases and more.

VIRTUAL MACHINE: A virtualized computing space produced by virtualization, mimicking a full physical computer system. It operates on its own with its operating system and apps.

WORKLOAD MANAGEMENT: Overseeing the efficient execution of tasks and processes within the cloud system, including prioritization, resource assignment and progress monitoring.

## CHAPTER THREE

Cloud service providers

Cloud service providers play a crucial role in delivering cloud computing services by offering a variety of cloud-based solutions, including storage, computing power and software applications, to both individuals and organizations. These providers are responsible for operating and maintaining the necessary infrastructure to enable users to conveniently and efficiently access and utilize cloud resources. In this chapter, we will explore the significance of cloud service providers in cloud computing, examining major players. We will compare their offerings, discuss considerations for selecting the right provider and explore concepts of vendor lock-in and interoperability.

Major cloud service providers

The world has seen the rise of significant companies that provide cloud services. These companies offer various services and technologies to meet the different needs of people all around the globe. In this section we will look at some of the top cloud service providers, such as AWS, GCP and Microsoft Azure.

Amazon Web Services

AWS was started in 2006 by Amazon. It has since gained significant popularity and has become a dominant force in the cloud services market. AWS provides a wide range of services that cater to the diverse needs of businesses and individuals, offering several advantages and benefits.

One of the key advantages of AWS is its extensive service offerings. It provides a comprehensive suite of cloud services, including computing power, storage options, databases, networking capabilities, analytics tools, artificial intelligence, machine learning and more. This wide array of services allows users to build, deploy and manage their applications and systems in a flexible and scalable manner.

Another notable advantage of AWS is its global infrastructure. AWS has multiple regions and availability zones spread across the world. This global footprint allows users to deploy their applications and store their data closer to their target audience, reducing latency and improving performance. Additionally, AWS offers a high level of reliability and uptime, ensuring that applications and services are available and accessible to users at all times.

AWS also stands out in terms of scalability. It provides the ability to scale computing resources up or down based on demand. This elasticity allows businesses to easily adjust their infrastructure to accommodate changes in workload and handle spikes in traffic.

When it comes to pricing, AWS offers a variety of models and options. Users can choose pay-as-you-go, where they pay for the resources they consume, or opt for reserved instances, which provide discounted rates for long-term commitments. AWS also offers spot instances, which allow users to bid on unused computing capacity for even greater cost savings.

Google Cloud Platform

GCP is a cloud computing platform provided by Google. It's another popular choice for businesses and individuals who want to use the cloud for their computing needs. GCP offers a variety of services and features that can help users with different aspects of cloud computing. You can use GCP to store your files and data, run your applications and use databases to organize your information. GCP also offers tools for analysing data, using artificial intelligence and learning from data to make predictions. It's like having a powerful computer in the cloud that you can use for all your computing tasks.

GCP also has a global infrastructure. Google has data centres located in different regions around the world. This means you can choose where to store your data and run your applications. Having data centres in different places allows for faster access to your information, as you can place it closer to where your users are located.

When it comes to pricing, GCP offers various options to fit different budgets. You can pay for the resources you use, so you only pay for what you actually need. GCP also provides cost management tools to help you keep track of your spending and optimize your usage to save money.

Another notable aspect of GCP is its emphasis on innovation. Google has a strong focus on artificial intelligence and machine learning, and GCP provides services and tools to incorporate these technologies into your applications. This can help you build intelligent and innovative apps.

Microsoft Azure

Microsoft Azure is a cloud computing platform created by Microsoft in 2010. It also helps people and businesses store and manage their data and applications on the internet instead of on their own computers. Azure offers a wide range of tools and services to make it easier for people to use the cloud.

With Azure, you can do things like create virtual machines to run your software, store your files and data in the cloud and use databases to organize and manage your information. Azure also has tools for analysing data, using artificial intelligence and learning from data to make predictions.

One of the cool things about Azure is that it works well with Microsoft's other products, like Office 365 and Dynamics 365. This means you can easily use Azure with the software you already know and use every day. It also gives you the option to connect your computers and systems to Azure, so you can have the best of both worlds – your computers and the power of the cloud.

Azure has data centres all around the world, so you can choose where to store your data and run your applications. This helps make sure your information is close to the people who need to use it, which makes things faster and more reliable.

When it comes to pricing, Azure has different options as well. You can pay for what you use, or you can get special pricing if you know you'll need a lot of resources for a long time. Azure also has cost management tools to help you keep track of how much you're spending and find ways to save money.

Other cloud providers

Beyond AWS, GCP and Microsoft Azure, there are other notable cloud service providers in the market. These providers offer different cloud services for various reasons. They have their own specialties and focus on specific industries or regions.

Some providers are known for their expertise in serving particular industries like healthcare, finance, emerging technologies or government. They understand the unique needs of these industries and provide cloud solutions tailored to them. Other providers focus on specific geographic areas, ensuring that data centres are located in those regions and comply with local laws and regulations.

Some cloud providers specialize in specific technologies like high-performance computing, data analytics, or the Internet of Things (IoT). They have advanced capabilities in these areas and offer specialized services to businesses that require such technologies.

There are also cloud providers that target small and medium-sized businesses. They offer cost-effective solutions and user-friendly interfaces, making it easier for smaller organizations to adopt cloud services.

Security and data privacy are also priorities for certain providers. They have enhanced measures in place to protect sensitive information and ensure that data is kept private and secure.

It's important to explore beyond the well-known providers and consider these alternative cloud service providers. By doing so, you can find the right fit for your specific needs and take advantage of specialized services that meet their requirements. Evaluating factors like service offerings, pricing, scalability, reliability and customer support will help you make an informed decision.

Here's a brief overview of some additional cloud providers:

- *Alibaba Cloud:* Alibaba Cloud is the cloud computing arm of Alibaba Group, a leading Chinese e-commerce company. It offers a wide range of cloud services, targeting both domestic and international markets. Alibaba Cloud specializes in serving global businesses and provides services such as computing, storage, networking, big data analytics and artificial intelligence (AI).
- *Cisco Cloud:* Cisco has a cloud platform known as Cisco Cloud Services and they have different infrastructure and networking services. It focuses on secure connectivity and integration with Cisco's networking and security solutions. Cisco Cloud helps businesses optimize their networks and manage workloads in a multicloud environment.
- *DigitalOcean:* DigitalOcean focuses on providing simple and affordable cloud infrastructure for developers and small

businesses. It offers scalable virtual machines called Droplets and a range of managed services, making it easier for users to deploy and scale applications. DigitalOcean is popular among developers for its user-friendly interface and cost-effective pricing options.

- *IBM Cloud:* IBM offers a cloud platform known as IBM Cloud, which provides a range of infrastructure, platform and software services. It emphasizes security, hybrid cloud capabilities and integration with IBM's extensive enterprise solutions. IBM Cloud offers AI-powered services, blockchain technology and other kinds of solutions that you can explore.
- *Oracle Cloud:* Oracle Cloud offers a comprehensive set of cloud services, including infrastructure, platform and software services. It focuses on delivering enterprise-grade solutions and provides tools for data management, artificial intelligence and machine learning. Oracle Cloud also offers specialized services for databases, applications and customer experience.
- *OVHcloud:* OVHcloud is a European cloud provider that offers public, private and hybrid cloud solutions. It focuses on data privacy and security and provides services for infrastructure, storage, networking and AI. OVHcloud operates its own global network and has data centres in Europe, North America and Asia.
- *Red Hat OpenShift:* Red Hat OpenShift is a container platform that enables developers to build, deploy and manage applications across hybrid cloud environments. It focuses on open-source technologies and provides enterprise-grade support. Red Hat OpenShift is widely used for containerization and application development.
- *Salesforce Cloud:* Salesforce is well-known for its CRM software, but it also has a cloud platform called Salesforce Cloud. It provides tools and services for building and deploying applications, managing customer relationships and automating business processes.

- *Tencent Cloud:* Tencent Cloud also has a wide range of cloud computing services and solutions. It specializes in serving businesses in China and provides services such as computing, storage, networking, AI and IoT. Tencent Cloud is known for its strong security measures and reliable performance.
- *Verizon Cloud:* Verizon offers cloud services, including computing, storage and networking capabilities. It caters to enterprises and provides secure, scalable and flexible solutions with a focus on network connectivity. Verizon Cloud supports various workloads and offers managed services to simplify cloud operations.
- *VMware Cloud:* VMware Cloud is a cloud infrastructure platform that leverages VMware's virtualization technology. It allows businesses to extend their existing on-premises infrastructure to the cloud and this helps create a seamless hybrid cloud experience. VMware Cloud offers features like workload migration, disaster recovery and unified management across public and private clouds.

Choosing the right cloud service provider

The decision of choosing the right cloud service provider is crucial and can have a big impact on how well your business does in the cloud. By carefully looking at these key factors, you can make a smart choice that matches what you need, makes your operations run smoothly, keeps your data safe and follows the rules, and lets your business grow and innovate using the full power of the cloud.

The key areas to evaluate before making a decision are as follows:

- *Service offerings:* When you're trying to choose a cloud service provider, it's important to look at the different services they offer. Find a provider with a wide variety of services that match what you need. These services can include things like computing power, storage space, databases to store your data, ways to connect and communicate between different parts of your system, keeping your data secure, tools to analyse and understand your data, using artificial intelligence and machine learning to make your software smarter, connecting devices in the IoT and tools that help you develop your software. Make sure the provider you choose has the services that fit your specific requirements.

- *Scalability and performance:* It's important to think about how well they can handle fluctuating workload demands. Sometimes your software might need to do a lot of work and other times it might not need to do much at all. You want a provider that can easily adjust the resources they give you to match your varying workload. It's also a good idea to check where the provider's data centres are located around the world. If the data centres are in close proximity with the people who will be using your software, it can make your software work faster because the information doesn't have to travel as far. This is called 'latency'. So, it's a good idea to make sure the provider has data centres in places that are close to your users. This can make your software perform better and make people happier when they use it.

- *Reliability:* It's important to see how often their systems are up and running without any problems. This is called 'uptime' and it means that your software and services are available to users when they need them. Choose a provider that has a good track record of keeping their systems running smoothly. It's also a good idea to look for providers that promise to have their systems available most of the time. This is called 'high availability guarantees'. It means that they work hard to make sure their systems are always up and running. Additionally, you should check whether the provider has plans in place to handle problems. This includes having systems that can keep working even if something goes wrong. This is called fault tolerance. It's also important to make sure the provider has plans for recovering quickly if there is a major problem like a natural disaster. All of these things are important because they help make sure your software and services have as little disruption as possible, which is really important for your users.

- *Security and compliance:* Data protection is very important. Make sure providers have good security measures in place. This means things like making sure your information is kept secure with strong encryption. Another thing to check is how they control who can access your data. They should have strict access controls, which means only authorized people can get to your information. It's also a good idea to find out whether the provider follows certain rules and regulations that are important for your industry or where you're located. For example, if you handle people's personal health information, they should follow rules like the US Health Insurance Portability and Accountability Act of 1996 (HIPAA). If you handle people's credit card information, they should follow rules like the Payment Card Industry Data Security Standard (PCI DSS). By checking these things, you can make sure your data is safe and that the provider follows the important rules and regulations that are needed to protect it.

- *Data sovereignty:* If you care about your data staying within a specific country or region, you should check whether the cloud service provider has data centres in those regions you want to exist in. This is called 'data sovereignty'. It means you have control over where your data is stored. You should also find out whether the provider offers options for where your data can be stored and whether they have clear rules for how they handle your data. This is important because different countries have different rules about how data should be protected and stored. So, it's a good idea to make sure the provider follows the specific rules that are important to you. By doing this, you can make sure your data stays where you want it to be and that the provider follows the important rules and regulations for handling your information.

- *Integration and interoperability:* When you're checking out different cloud service providers, it's really important to find out whether they work well with the systems, applications and tools you're already using. Make sure they can easily work together. One thing to consider is whether the provider supports industry standards. These are like a set of rules that different software and systems follow, so they can work together smoothly. You should also consider their support for APIs and integration capabilities with other cloud services, on-premises infrastructure, or third-party services. By checking all these things, you can make sure the provider will work well with what you already have and that everything will run smoothly when you use their cloud services.
- *Performance monitoring and management:* It's also very important to think about the tools and features they give you to monitor and manage your resources. Make sure you have everything you need to manage them effectively. One thing to look for is a monitoring dashboard that shows you information about how your resources are performing. It helps you keep an eye on things and make sure everything is running smoothly. It's also a good idea to find out whether the provider has automated scaling. This means that they can automatically adjust the amount of resources you have based on how much work your software needs to do. It helps ensure you always have enough resources to handle the workload. Another thing to check for is resource optimization. This means that the provider helps you use your resources in the best possible way, so you're not wasting anything. You should also look for logging features. This means that the provider keeps a record of what's happening with your resources. It can be really helpful when you need to troubleshoot or when you want to improve the performance of your software.
- *Pricing:* When you're deciding on a cloud service provider, it's important to look at the pricing for using their services. Establish how much it will cost and whether there are ways to

save money. One thing to think about is how they price their services based on what you use. This is called 'on-demand pricing'. It means you pay for what you use, like paying for electricity based on how much you use it. Another thing to consider is reserved instances. This is like making a reservation in advance. You commit to using certain resources for a longer time and you get a discount on the price. Spot instances are also worth considering. These are cheaper resources that become available when there is less demand. However, the provider can take them away if they need them for other customers. Lastly, it's also good to check whether the provider offers cost management tools to help you track and control your spending. These tools help you track how much you're spending and find ways to save money.

- *Support and service level agreements (SLAs):* Support means having a team of experts who can help you when you have questions or run into problems. Make sure that the provider you choose has support available all the time, 24/7, so you can get help whenever you need it. It's also important to consider how quickly they respond to your requests and how long it takes them to solve the issues you're facing. Another thing to look at is their SLAs. These are like contracts that outline the promises the provider makes about their services. You should review the SLAs to find out whether they guarantee a certain amount of uptime, which means your services will be available and not experiencing any downtime. If there are any disruptions and they don't meet the uptime guarantees, they might offer service credits or compensation to make up for it. On the other hand, there might be penalties for the provider if they don't fulfil their promises.

- *Community:* When you're considering a cloud service provider, it's important to look at the vibrancy of their community. This means seeing how many people use their services and how active they are in sharing knowledge and helping each other. A big and lively community means there are lots of resources available for you to learn from, get support when you need it and collaborate with others who are using the same services. It's also worth checking whether the provider has user groups or forums where users can ask questions and find answers. These resources can be really helpful when you're stuck or want to learn more about how to use certain features.

- *Reputation and longevity:* You should make sure that the cloud provider you're considering has a good track record of providing quality services and that other customers have had positive experiences with them. One way to check this is by looking at customer reviews and seeing what other people have to say about their services. It's also important to consider the long-term viability of the provider. Make sure that they will be around for a long time. This is important, because if a provider goes out of business or stops offering their services it can cause a lot of disruption for you and your applications. Another thing to look at is the provider's commitment to innovation and future growth. Make sure that they are actively working on improving their services and staying up-to-date with the latest technologies. It's also helpful to find out whether they have partnerships with other companies or organizations, as this can indicate their commitment to collaboration and expanding their offerings.
- *Geographical coverage and regional support:* When you're deciding on a cloud service provider, it's important to think about where they have their presence and how well they can support you in the regions where you work or want to expand. Make sure that they have enough coverage and that they have support teams located in those regions to help you with your specific needs and any regulations that you have to follow. Having a local presence means that the provider has data centres or offices in the areas where you operate. This can be important because it can help reduce delays and improve performance since the data doesn't have to travel long distances. It's also helpful to have support teams in those

regions because they will be familiar with the local requirements and can provide assistance that is tailored to your specific location.

- *Organizational alignment:* It's important to evaluate how
well they match your business's goals, culture and strategic
direction. Make sure that their vision and plans align with
what you want to achieve. You can consider their commitment to customer success, which means how dedicated they
are to helping their customers achieve their goals and be successful in using their services.

- *Contractual and legal considerations:* Carefully read and understand their terms of service, contracts and legal obliga-
tions. These documents outline important details that you
should be aware of. It's important to understand the termination clauses in the contract. These clauses explain what happens if you want to stop using the provider's services or if they
want to end the agreement. Make sure that the terms are fair
and that you have a clear understanding of the process.

Vendor lock-in and interoperability

When making a decision about which cloud service provider to
choose, it's important to keep in mind that the choice you make
now may not necessarily be the best choice for your business as
it scales and grows. And that's okay. As your business evolves,
your needs may change and you might require different services
or features that your current provider may not offer.

One challenge that can arise as your business scales is vendor
lock-in. Vendor lock-in happens when a business becomes too
dependent on one cloud service provider and finds it hard to
switch to another provider or make changes to their cloud setup.
This can occur because of things like special technologies,
custom ways of connecting to other systems, specific ways of
storing data, or complicated integrations that only work with

that provider. Being locked in like this limits a business's ability to try out and use new ideas and services from other providers that might be better or cheaper. It can also be expensive and disruptive to switch to a different provider. Plus, the chosen provider might have plans that don't match what the business needs in the future.

To avoid the problems of vendor lock-in, interoperability is key. Interoperability means that different systems, programs and platforms can all work together smoothly. In the case of cloud services, it means that the technologies, ways of connecting to other systems and data formats used by one provider can work with those of other providers or even with systems a business runs on its own. Paying attention to interoperability helps a business keep its flexibility and freedom to choose. It makes it possible to combine different systems and use them together easily, so everything can work well and information can be shared without any problems. By using common standards, similar ways of connecting to systems and the best ways of doing things in the industry, a business can avoid getting stuck with only one provider and be ready to switch to another if it needs to.

Having interoperability is also important for being able to try out new ideas and use new services. A business can take advantage of the special things different providers offer, like services that are great for certain tasks or new technologies that are just starting out. It also makes it easy to work with partners, customers, or other systems owned by other people, so information can flow between them smoothly and they can all work together well.

REVIEW

In this chapter, we covered some prominent cloud service providers and the crucial factors to take into account when selecting the ideal one for your business. The concept of vendor lock-in was also introduced, explaining the challenges of being tied to a specific provider. Now, armed with this knowledge, you can confidently make choices that suit your business needs and plans.

Understanding the offerings of different cloud service providers helps us compare their features, costs and how well they fit the needs of the business or product. You now know how important scalability, data security and customer support are when choosing a provider. Plus, you've learned strategies to reduce the risks of vendor lock-in by using standard technologies and methods to move your data. By knowing the downsides of vendor lock-in, you can negotiate better terms and find ways to move your data if needed. This chapter gives you a toolbox to pick the right cloud service provider for your business while considering growth and avoiding problems tied to vendor lock-in.

GLOSSARY

COMMUNITY: The user community associated with a specific cloud service provider. A vibrant community provides resources, support and collaboration opportunities for users to share knowledge and best practices.

DATA CENTRE: A facility equipped with servers, storage devices and networking equipment used to house and manage computing resources for cloud services.

DATA SOVEREIGNTY: The concept of having control over where data is stored and processed, often driven by legal and regulatory requirements.

INTEGRATION: The process of making different systems, applications and services work together seamlessly.

INTEROPERABILITY: The ability of different systems, software and platforms to work seamlessly together. In the context of cloud computing, interoperability ensures that various cloud services, technologies and data formats can interact and collaborate effectively.

PRICING MODELS: Different approaches to charging customers for using cloud services.

REPUTATION: The perception and assessment of a cloud service provider's reliability, performance and customer satisfaction. A provider's reputation can influence the decision-making process for businesses choosing a cloud partner.

SERVICE LEVEL AGREEMENT (SLA): A contract between a cloud service provider and its customers that outlines the agreed-upon level of service, including uptime guarantees, support response times and penalties or compensations for service disruptions.

VENDOR LOCK-IN: A situation in which a business becomes overly dependent on a single cloud service provider, making it difficult to switch to another provider or adapt to changing needs.

## CHAPTER FOUR

Cloud storage

Cloud storage and data management are important in technology today. They have the potential to really change the way we store, access and manage our valuable data. This chapter will explore the amazing benefits they offer and discover the various storage options available to cater to your unique needs. We'll also discuss how to keep your data safe and secure, explore strategies for backup and disaster recovery and provide practical tips for effective data management.

Understanding cloud storage

Cloud storage has completely changed the way we store and manage data. In the past, we relied on physical devices like hard drives and tapes to store our data. However, these devices had limitations in terms of storage capacity, expandability and accessibility. But with the advent of cloud storage, everything changed for the better. Cloud storage uses the internet and a technology called virtualization to allow us to store our data on remote servers. This means we can access our data from anywhere using the internet without the need for physical devices. This shift eliminates the constraints of physical storage and offers numerous benefits.

It provides unlimited space to store our data without any worries of running out of storage capacity. All that matters is that you pay for your storage space. This is possible because cloud storage uses special remote servers that can be easily adjusted to accommodate the amount of data we have. Whether we need a little space or a lot, the cloud can expand or shrink to fit our needs, ensuring that we always have enough room to store all our important files and information.

With cloud storage, we have the freedom to access our data from anywhere using different devices like computers, smartphones or tablets, as long as we have an internet connection. This means we can get to our files and information whenever we need them, whether we're at home, in the office, or anywhere else. It's not just about accessing our data, but also sharing it with others. With cloud storage, we can easily share files and folders with specific people, allowing them to see and work on the same files as us. This makes working together on projects much easier because different people in different locations using different devices can collaborate and make changes to the same files at the same time.

Cloud service providers implement measures to keep our data safe and secure. They use techniques like encryption and authentication to make sure only authorized people can access our data. With cloud storage, you can trust that your data is protected and secure. They also create additional copies of our data in different locations, so even if something bad happens to one location, we still have our data safe in other locations. They have plans in place to handle hardware problems or unexpected disasters, so our data is always protected. They also create copies of our data and store them in many different places – this is a term in distributed services called 'replication'. This way, even if something goes wrong with one storage location, we won't lose our data. It gives us peace of mind knowing that our data is protected and reliable.

Cloud storage models

Cloud storage models are the different options or methods available for storing and organizing your files online. Each model has its own features and benefits that you can choose from. You can decide how much control you want over your files, how secure you want them to be, how easily you can expand your storage and how much it will cost you.

Knowing about these different models helps you make informed decisions about which one is best for you. You might want to collaborate with others, keep your files private, or have the flexibility to access your documents from anywhere. Regardless of the goal, cloud storage models offer different options for various needs. There are four main cloud storage models: public, private, hybrid and community.

Public cloud storage

Public cloud storage is a very popular option for storing data. It's offered by companies like Amazon Web Services, Microsoft Azure and Google Cloud Platform. These companies provide storage space to the public through the internet.

To explain cloud storage, let's assume that public cloud services are like large shared lockers. Imagine a locker room where all your classmates, including you, have access to lockers provided by a trusted third-party contracted by your school. While the lockers are in the same room and managed by the provider, each locker is secure and can only be accessed by the person who owns it (except, of course, if you leave it open without a password or access control mechanisms – now everyone will have access to it).

Similarly, in public cloud storage, service providers offer access to their cloud infrastructure to multiple organizations and individuals. You can think of it as renting a digital locker for your applications and data. Although the infrastructure is shared among different users, your specific data and applications are kept separate and can only be accessed by you. It's like having your own private locker within a shared locker room.

Public cloud storage has many advantages. It is cost-effective because you don't have to invest in and maintain your own storage infrastructure. It also provides scalability, allowing you to easily expand or reduce your storage capacity based on what you need. Public cloud storage also offers accessibility, which allows you to access your data and applications from anywhere with an internet connection.

However, it's important to consider data security and privacy when using public cloud storage. While your data is protected and isolated within your digital locker, it resides alongside other users' data within the same shared infrastructure. Therefore, it's essential to choose a reputable and reliable service provider that implements strong security measures to ensure the safety of your data.

Private cloud storage

While public cloud storage is like renting a locker in a shared locker room, private cloud storage is more like having your own personal locker room.

In private cloud storage, the cloud infrastructure is dedicated exclusively to one organization. This ensures that your data and applications are kept separate and secure.

With private cloud storage, organizations have full control over their cloud resources. They can customize the storage environment according to their specific needs and set their own security measures to protect their data.

One of the main advantages of private cloud storage is the added layer of security and privacy it provides. Since the infrastructure is dedicated solely to one organization, there is less risk of data breaches or unauthorized access.

Private cloud storage is especially useful for organizations that deal with sensitive or confidential data and need extra security measures. It also offers predictable and consistent performance, making it ideal for critical applications that require high availability.

However, setting up and managing a private cloud can be more complex and costly compared to using the public cloud. It requires expertise and investment in hardware, software and maintenance.

Hybrid cloud storage

Hybrid cloud storage is a blend of public and private cloud storage, offering the best of both worlds. Imagine you have access to two locker rooms: one that is shared with your classmates (public cloud storage) and another that is exclusively yours (private cloud storage). Hybrid cloud storage combines these two locker rooms, allowing you to store some of your items in the shared locker and others in your private locker.

In hybrid cloud storage, organizations can choose to store certain data and applications in a public cloud environment while keeping other sensitive or critical data in a private cloud environment.

This flexibility provides several benefits. It allows organizations to take advantage of the cost-effectiveness and scalability of the public cloud for less sensitive data, while also benefiting from the added security and control of the private cloud for more critical data.

For example, a company might use the public cloud to store and process non-sensitive data like marketing materials or public-facing websites. At the same time, they might use a private cloud for confidential customer data, financial records, or proprietary business applications.

Hybrid cloud storage also offers seamless data movement between the two environments. Data can be securely transferred and integrated between the public and private clouds, ensuring that the right data is available to the right users at the right time.

This combination of public and private cloud storage provides organizations with greater flexibility, allowing them to optimize their storage resources based on their specific needs and requirements.

However, managing a hybrid cloud environment can be more complex than using either public or private cloud storage alone. It requires careful planning, integration and coordination between the two environments.

Community cloud storage

Community cloud storage is another option. It's like a shared locker room where a specific group of people, like members of a community or organization, have access to a dedicated set of lockers.

Imagine you are part of a special club at your gym and your club members have access to a separate locker room just for your club. It caters to the needs of a specific community or group of users.

In community cloud storage, multiple organizations or individuals with similar interests, goals or security requirements come together to share cloud infrastructure and resources. This creates a more focused and tailored environment for them.

For instance, in the healthcare industry different healthcare providers may form a community cloud to share medical records and collaborate on patient care. They can access and store data within this specialized cloud environment while adhering to strict healthcare regulations and data privacy requirements.

Community cloud storage offers several benefits. By sharing resources and costs across a community, it can be more cost-effective than setting up individual private clouds.

However, just like any other cloud storage model, community cloud storage also requires careful planning and management. Members of the community must establish clear guidelines and agreements regarding resource usage, security measures and data sharing practices.

DIFFERENCES BETWEEN PUBLIC AND COMMUNITY CLOUD STORAGE

This section highlights the differences between public and community cloud storage according to user types, resource sharing and security.

User types

- *Public cloud storage:* Public cloud storage is like a one-size-fits-all option for cloud services. It offers a lot of different services and features, but it may not be tailor-made for specific industries or groups of users with unique needs. Instead, it provides a standard set of services that can work for many different types of users.

- *Community cloud storage:* Community cloud storage is like a special club where people with similar interests, goals or security needs come together. They work as a team and share a common storage space in the cloud to meet their needs. For instance, think of a group of teachers from different schools who want to share educational resources, lesson plans and student data. Instead of each school managing its own storage, they create a community cloud where all the teachers can access and store their teaching materials securely. This way, they can work together more efficiently and share valuable resources for better education outcomes.

Resource sharing

- *Public cloud storage:* Public cloud storage involves sharing cloud infrastructure among multiple users, but these users are typically not part of the same community. Resource sharing is based on a multitenant model, where different customers share the same infrastructure without direct collaboration.

- *Community cloud storage:* Community cloud storage fosters collaboration and resource sharing among its members. The community members work together to optimize resource utilization and cost-sharing, which can lead to enhanced efficiency and cost-effectiveness.

Security

- *Public cloud storage:* Although public cloud service providers have strong security measures, the way public cloud storage works involves multiple users sharing the same infrastructure. This can raise concerns for organizations about data separation and possible security risks when sharing resources with unknown users.

- *Community cloud storage:* In community cloud storage, the members have similar security needs, which means they can use special security measures that suit their specific industries. This focused security approach provides higher levels of protection and privacy for the data shared within the community.

Now that you know about the different ways data can be stored in the cloud, let's discover the various types of cloud storage. These types show us how data is kept, managed and accessed in the cloud. Understanding these storage types will help you better understand cloud computing and make smart choices when picking the right storage.

Types of cloud storage

Imagine you have a wide variety of items to store in the cloud, from documents and photos to videos and applications. There are different ways to organize and manage these items effectively. These methods are called cloud storage types.

Cloud storage types are like distinct containers (or buckets), each designed to hold specific types of items securely and efficiently. Just as you would choose a box, a folder or a jar based on what you want to store, cloud storage types offer specialized solutions for your data needs.

By understanding cloud storage types, you can efficiently manage and access your data in the cloud, just as you would choose the right container to organize and access your belongings in real life. Whether you are a student organizing your assignments, a software engineer storing different programming books, or a business handling massive amounts of data, the right cloud storage type ensures your data is kept safe, organized and easily accessible. There are three main cloud storage types: block, file and object.

Block storage

Block storage is a technology commonly used to store data files in cloud-based storage environments or on storage area networks (SANs). In the cloud, block storage is often achieved by attaching a virtual disk to a cloud-based virtual machine.

In this approach, data is divided into smaller pieces called 'blocks', each with a unique identifier. This allows the storage system to efficiently place these blocks in the best location. The blocks can be stored across different systems and each block can work with different operating systems, such as Linux or Windows.

Block storage offers the advantage of separating data from your personal environment, allowing it to be spread across multiple environments. This creates multiple paths to access the data, making data retrieval faster. When you or an application request data from a block storage system, the storage system gathers all the necessary blocks, re-assembles them and then presents the complete data back to you.

APPLICATIONS OF BLOCK STORAGE

Block storage is commonly used for various applications and scenarios. Here are several practical examples that highlight the wide-ranging utility of block storage in different scenarios:

- *Virtual machines (VMs):* In cloud computing, block storage is frequently used in virtual machines, offering long-lasting storage for applications and data. VMs can utilize block storage to house operating systems, software and other essential data required for smooth application execution.
- *Databases:* Block storage is a great choice for databases, as it stores data in predefined blocks of a fixed size. This arrangement facilitates rapid and direct access to particular data blocks, making it ideal for database operations involving frequent read and write actions.
- *High-performance computing:* In high-performance computing environments, block storage is used to store large datasets and execute data-intensive applications. This ensures fast access and efficient processing of data, which is crucial for scientific simulations, data analytics and research projects.
- *Content delivery networks (CDNs):* CDNs use block storage to cache and distribute static content, such as images, videos and web pages. By storing these assets in blocks, CDNs can quickly deliver content to users, reducing latency and improving website performance.
- *Backup and disaster recovery:* Block storage is often used in backup and disaster recovery solutions, allowing organizations to create regular snapshots of data and restore it quickly if they experience data loss or system failures.

File storage

In cloud storage, file storage follows a hierarchical method of data organization, often called file-level or file-based storage. Data is stored in files, which are then organized into folders, directories and subdirectories. To find and access a specific file, users and applications must follow the pathway from the directory down to the desired folder and file. This essential information is stored as metadata, which is attached to the file.

File storage offers a wide range of capabilities, making it suitable for storing various types of data. Just like with a regular computer, you can store complex files and navigating through them is generally fast and straightforward. The configuration process is also simple, allowing you to control access to files using user rights, file locking and other features.

However, as your file storage grows larger, you may encounter performance issues, especially in file retrieval. This slowdown is due to the limitation of having only one pathway to each file, which becomes more problematic as you add more folders, directories and subdirectories.

To address these performance concerns, cloud systems offer solutions. You can scale your storage by including higher-capacity virtual machines with additional compute power. Nonetheless, it's essential to consider that this approach may be less efficient and more expensive compared to choosing an object or block storage method.

APPLICATIONS OF FILE STORAGE

File storage is a versatile and essential component of the digital landscape, catering to a wide range of storage needs for individuals, businesses and various cloud applications. Here are some practical examples that highlight the use of file storage in different scenarios:

- *File sharing and collaboration:* Cloud-based file storage platforms allow users to share files and collaborate with others instantly. Examples of such services are Google Drive, Dropbox and Microsoft OneDrive. Everyone can effortlessly upload, store and distribute files with colleagues, clients or friends.

- *Document management:* File storage is frequently utilized for document management in various businesses and organizations. It enables users to store and arrange files, simplifying access and management of crucial documents. Document management systems, such as SharePoint and Box, offer file storage functionalities designed specifically for business needs.

- *Multimedia storage:* File storage is employed to keep various media content, including photos, videos and music files. Users have the option to store their media files on cloud-based services like iCloud, Amazon Cloud Drive or Flickr, guaranteeing secure storage and convenient access from multiple devices.

- *Web hosting:* File storage is frequently used to store website files, which encompass HTML pages, scripts, images and other resources. Web hosting providers present file storage solutions to host website files, enabling users worldwide to access them through the internet.

- *Backup and archiving:* File storage can also be used for backup and archiving purposes. Cloud-based backup services are used by businesses and individuals to store duplicates of essential files and data, offering safeguarding against data loss due to hardware issues, accidents, or security breaches.

- *Software deployment:* File storage systems are used to store software applications and updates. Software developers and companies utilize file storage to distribute applications, ensuring users can conveniently download and install the software.

- *Personal data organization:* File storage provides a convenient method for people to arrange their personal data, such as personal documents, resumes and other files. Users have the option to create folders and subfolders to categorize their files, making it simple to find and access them whenever needed.

Object storage

Object storage is an advanced data management method that involves segmenting data files into discrete units called objects. These objects are stored in a centralized repository but can be distributed across multiple cloud-based servers and interconnected systems. Object storage can be used to store unstructured data as 'objects'. Examples of object storage services are Azure Storage, Cloudflare R2 Storage and Amazon S3.

Each object is assigned a unique identifier and this helps with seamless retrieval. Object storage also incorporates essential metadata that carries critical information such as object size, modification timestamps, media format and access permissions.

The flat architecture of object storage is highly efficient for accommodating vast amounts of data. Its versatility extends to storing various types of data, including multimedia files, documents and system logs. This robust and scalable approach empowers organizations to manage their data efficiently in cloud-based environments, ensuring optimal organization, security and accessibility of critical information.

APPLICATIONS OF OBJECT STORAGE

Object storage is widely used for various purposes in modern computing. These practical examples highlight the use of object storage in different scenarios:

- *Cloud backup and archiving:* A lot of cloud backup and archiving platforms, like Amazon S3 (Simple Storage Service) and Google Cloud Storage, make use of object storage. Users can securely save backups of their files, databases and entire systems in the cloud, ensuring data protection and straightforward recovery in case of any data loss.
- *Content distribution:* Content delivery networks make use of object storage to effectively distribute and cache content, like images, videos and website assets, across various geographic

locations. This enhances website performance and minimizes latency for users accessing the content.

- *Social media and photo sharing platforms:* Social media platforms such as Facebook, Instagram and Flickr utilize object storage to store and deliver millions of photos and videos uploaded by users all around the globe. Object storage enables seamless access and sharing of multimedia content.
- *Genome sequencing and scientific research:* In scientific research, object storage is utilized to store and analyse substantial datasets, such as genomic data, astronomical observations and climate simulations.
- *IoT data management:* IoT devices produce massive volumes of data. Object storage is employed to effectively store and handle this data in a scalable and economical way, facilitating streamlined analysis and decision-making processes.
- *Data analytics and big data:* Object storage plays a vital role in storing unstructured data, such as log files, sensor data and machine-generated information, that is subsequently utilized for big data analytics and data mining purposes.
- *Media and entertainment:* Media companies, streaming services and video hosting platforms make use of object storage to handle extensive media files, facilitating smooth streaming and efficient content delivery to their users.
- *Cloud-native applications:* Cloud-native applications developed with microservices architecture leverage object storage as a scalable and robust data repository to manage substantial amounts of user-generated content and application data.

Cloud storage providers

Cloud storage providers are companies that offer storage solutions in the cloud to people, businesses and organizations. These companies run big data centres where they provide storage space through the internet. This lets users store, organize and get their data from anywhere. Cloud storage providers offer various ways to store data, like block storage, file storage and object storage, so people can choose the best one for their needs.

Some popular cloud storage providers are:

- *Amazon Web Services:* AWS offers a service called Amazon S3 (Simple Storage Service), which is an object storage solution that can grow as needed and is very reliable. AWS also has the Elastic Block Store (EBS) for block storage and Amazon EFS (Elastic File System) for file storage.
- *Microsoft Azure:* In Microsoft Azure, there is a storage service called Azure Blob Storage. It's used for storing unstructured data, such as documents, images and videos. Azure Disk Storage, on the other hand, is designed for block storage, mainly for virtual machines and applications. For managed file sharing in the cloud Azure Files is available; and for message-based communication there's Azure Queue Storage. Microsoft Azure also offers Azure Archive Storage, which is ideal for retaining data for the long term.
- *Google Cloud Platform:* GCP provides a service called Google Cloud Storage, which is a very scalable way to store and access data in the cloud. For block storage requirements they offer Google Cloud Persistent Disk and if you need fully managed file storage there's Google Cloud Filestore.
- *Dropbox:* Dropbox is a cloud storage and file-syncing service primarily designed for individual users and small businesses. It has a user-friendly interface that makes it easy to store and share files across various devices. For teams and organizations, Dropbox Business offers extra features and collaboration tools.
- *iCloud:* iCloud is a cloud storage and synchronization service created by Apple, mainly for users of Apple devices. With iCloud, users can store documents, photos, videos and app data in the cloud, ensuring that all their Apple devices stay in sync. It works seamlessly with iOS and macOS devices, offering a convenient storage solution for those within the Apple ecosystem.

Every provider offers a variety of features, pricing options and service levels, allowing users to select the best fit for their needs and budget.

Using cloud storage providers comes with numerous advantages. They eliminate the need for users to invest in and manage their physical storage infrastructure, resulting in cost savings and less IT management work. Users can easily expand or reduce their storage resources as required, providing both flexibility and cost-effectiveness. These companies also have robust security measures to protect user data, guaranteeing that sensitive information stays safe and cannot be accessed by unauthorized identities. With numerous data centres and redundant storage systems, cloud storage providers ensure that data is highly accessible and durable, minimizing the chances of data loss caused by hardware malfunctions.

REVIEW

This chapter covered cloud storage, including the different cloud storage types and cloud storage models.

There are three main types of cloud storage: object storage, file storage and block storage. These types help you store and manage your data in different ways. We also explored four models for cloud storage: private, public, hybrid and community clouds. These models help you decide how you want to control and access your stored data.

Understanding these ideas can help you choose the best way to store and manage your important information in the cloud.

GLOSSARY

ACCESSIBILITY: The ability to access stored data from various devices and locations using an internet connection. Cloud storage enables remote access to data, promoting flexibility and convenience.

BACKUP: Creating copies of data to be stored separately for recovery in case the original data is lost or damaged. Cloud storage often includes automated backup services.

CLOUD STORAGE: The practice of storing and managing data using remote servers accessed through the internet. It eliminates the need for physical storage devices and offers advantages like unlimited space, remote access and easy sharing of files.

CLOUD STORAGE TYPES: Different methods of organizing and managing data in cloud-based environments, tailored to specific data needs.

DATA CENTRES: Large facilities equipped with servers and storage systems where cloud storage providers store users' data securely and ensure its accessibility.

DATA MIGRATION: The process of transferring data from one storage environment to another, such as moving data from on-premises storage to cloud storage.

DATA REDUNDANCY: The practice of creating duplicate copies of data and storing them in different locations. Cloud storage providers use data redundancy to ensure data integrity and availability in case of hardware failures or disasters.

DISASTER RECOVERY: A strategy to restore data and operations in case of data loss or system failures due to natural disasters, cyber attacks or other emergencies.

STORAGE CAPACITY: The amount of data that can be held by a storage system. Cloud storage provides virtually unlimited storage capacity that can be adjusted according to user needs.

VIRTUALIZATION: A technology used in cloud storage to create virtual instances of computing resources, such as storage, networks and servers. It allows multiple virtual environments to run on a single physical hardware system.

## CHAPTER FIVE

Big data and analytics in the cloud

Big data and analytics in the cloud is an approach that combines the power of data insights with the flexibility of cloud technology, changing how businesses work. In this chapter, we'll explore this exciting blend in an easy-to-understand way. We'll cover big data's basics, how the cloud helps store and process vast datasets and the tools that make it happen.

We'll also explore data analytics and machine learning, understanding how they provide valuable insights for making informed decisions. By the end of this chapter, you will have seen how innovation and success can be driven by the potential of data and will understand the wide range of possibilities that big data and analytics in the cloud offer.

Introduction to big data

I learned about big data in 2015 when I took an IBM course. There, I was introduced to big data and its three Vs: volume, variety and velocity. The course introduced me to Hadoop and its ecosystem, including MapReduce for distributed data processing. I also explored Apache Spark, a faster and more versatile alternative to MapReduce (these may mean nothing to you at the moment, but I will introduce them later in the chapter). Data pre-processing and visualization techniques were also emphasized to ensure accurate insights. The experience taught me about big data and its potential to transform businesses and drive innovation.

So, what is big data?

With all the digital activities in our world today, we create a lot of data from many sources, like social media, online shopping and more. Some of this data doesn't have a clear structure, like pictures or videos. Making sense of all this information is important for understanding things better, as *data is how we make sense of the world*.

Big data is a term used for the huge and complex datasets we have nowadays. There's so much data that normal computer tools can't handle it all. Big data includes different types of information and it's generated very quickly.

To deal with big data, we use advanced technologies that help us store, process and analyse all this information efficiently. This allows us to find valuable patterns and insights that were hard to see before.

Using big data is crucial for businesses and other organizations to stay competitive, make more informed business decisions and discover new opportunities for growth and improvement. It's become an important part of how we understand and use the vast amount of data we have in our world today.

HOW BIG DATA WORKS

Big data as a farm

Imagine you are a farmer in charge of a massive vegetable farm. Every day, your farm produces a lot of different vegetables. To

---

handle all these vegetables efficiently, you should categorize them based on their unique characteristics.

In this analogy, the vegetables represent the data and managing the farm reflects the challenges of dealing with big data. Just like your farm produces a large number of vegetables daily, big data is vast and continuously generated from various sources like social media, sensors and more.

Each vegetable's unique characteristics symbolize the diverse types of data, including structured and unstructured information collected from different channels. To manage this abundance of data effectively, you need advanced tools and systems. Similarly, dealing with big data requires sophisticated technologies like distributed computing and analytics tools to store, process and extract valuable insights from the massive datasets.

The synergy between big data and cloud computing

Big data and cloud computing are two technologies that have a powerful synergy that unlocks the full potential of data-driven insights. Big data, with its three defining Vs – volume, variety and velocity – represents the vast and diverse datasets generated from countless sources every second. On the other hand, cloud computing provides an elastic and scalable infrastructure that offers access to a shared pool of computing resources over the internet. This combination proves to be a perfect match for managing and analysing all the data, enabling organizations to tap into invaluable insights.

Let's now see the specific reasons behind this synergy:

- *Flexible infrastructure:* The cloud provides a flexible and customizable infrastructure for businesses. Dealing with big data, which involves large datasets and changing workloads, makes this flexibility crucial. Organizations can easily adjust their computing power, storage capacity and networking resources based on their needs, ensuring they work efficiently and save costs.

- *Elastic data storage:* Storing and handling big data needs a lot of space and it can be expensive and complicated to manage it on-site. But cloud-based storage solutions like object storage and data lakes offer almost unlimited space to store huge datasets. Businesses can easily store and access their data in the cloud without worrying about hardware limitations or having to plan for capacity.

- *On-demand data processing:* In the cloud, organizations can use a pay-as-you-go model for data processing and analytics tasks. This means businesses can easily get the resources they need and run complex data processing tasks whenever necessary, without committing to long-term investments in infrastructure. With the option to create virtual machines or containerized environments, companies can perform complicated data operations efficiently and at a reasonable cost.

- *Global accessibility:* This is mostly useful to global organizations. With cloud computing, you can access data and analytics tools from anywhere in the world, making it easy for distributed teams to work together. This global accessibility means that people from different locations and time zones can use big data insights and analytics to make informed decisions throughout the organization.

- *Managed services:* Cloud providers offer services and platforms to manage big data, making it easier to set up and run complex data processing tasks. These services come with built-in security, reliability and scalability features, so organizations don't have to worry about managing the underlying infrastructure. Beyond these managed services, cloud providers have data experts who can help organizations improve their big data workflows and achieve better outcomes.

Challenges of big analytics in the cloud

Although there are a lot of benefits when using the cloud for big data analytics, it's essential to understand the challenges so that you are fully informed and can tap into the full potential of this technology.

One critical concern is data security. When data moves between different servers and geographical regions in the cloud, there's a chance that it could be vulnerable to attacks by hackers. Making sure sensitive data is secure becomes very important and organizations need to take steps like using encryption, access controls and multi-factor authentication to protect their information.

Data privacy is also very important. As rules about handling data get stricter, organizations must give high importance to data privacy when using the cloud. It's important to remember that various industries and regions have specific rules that organizations must follow when dealing with sensitive data. Making sure they follow data privacy laws like the General Data Protection Regulation (GDPR) in Europe and the California Consumer Privacy Act (CCPA) in the USA is crucial and organizations need to use techniques like data anonymization, pseudonymization and consent management to protect people's privacy rights. Complying with industry-specific regulations such as healthcare (HIPAA), financial services (PCI DSS) and government (the Federal Risk and Authorization Management Program (FedRAMP)) is vital to avoid legal repercussions. It's a good idea for organizations to work with cloud providers that have compliance certifications and get checked by outside experts regularly.

Managing data governance and maintaining data quality and consistency can also be challenging in the cloud, where data may reside in different regions or across various cloud services. Organizations need to put effective data governance systems in place to have complete control and see where their data is, no matter where it is stored.

With cyber threats always changing and becoming more sophisticated, organizations need to have continuous monitoring and plans to respond to any security breaches quickly. Using real-time threat detection, security monitoring tools and clear incident response protocols can help reduce risks effectively.

By understanding and addressing these challenges, organizations can fully unlock the power of cloud-based big data analytics in a safe and responsible way. This understanding gives businesses the ability to make informed decisions, foster innovation and achieve remarkable results using data-driven approaches.

Big data processing frameworks

Big data processing frameworks are advanced tools made to handle the huge and complex datasets that are common in the world of big data.

In this section, we will look at some of the most popular big data processing frameworks. These frameworks have changed how organizations analyse data and have made it possible to find important insights and patterns from big data. These frameworks use distributed computing and parallel processing to divide complex data tasks into smaller parts that can be processed at the same time on a group of connected computers. This helps make data processing more manageable and efficient.

Apache Hadoop

Apache Hadoop is a well-known tool for handling large and complex data. It's widely used by organizations dealing with massive amounts of data. It uses the Hadoop Distributed File System (HDFS), which stores data across multiple computers in a cluster. This storage system ensures data is safe and always available even if some computers fail.

Hadoop's strength lies in its ability to process data in parallel, meaning it can work on many parts of the data at the same time. It does this using a method called MapReduce, which splits data tasks into smaller pieces and processes them independently. After all the pieces are processed, the results are combined to get the final output. This makes Hadoop efficient in handling large-scale data processing tasks.

Hadoop is widely used for batch processing tasks like log analysis, data warehousing and data mining. It breaks down the tasks into smaller parts, reducing the time it takes to process data and giving valuable insights from large datasets that are difficult to analyse otherwise.

Apache Spark

Apache Spark has become famous for its impressive speed and versatility. Unlike Hadoop's MapReduce, Spark uses an in-memory approach to process data, making it work much faster. By keeping data in memory, Spark reduces the need for reading and writing data to disks frequently, which was a common slowdown in traditional data processing systems. This improvement in processing speed contributes to Spark's outstanding performance.

Spark is known for its ability to handle various data processing tasks, making it a flexible and multipurpose big data tool. Whether it's batch processing, real-time stream processing, machine learning or graph processing, Spark can handle a wide range of operations. This makes Spark a one-stop solution for many data-related tasks, allowing organizations to perform complex analyses and get valuable insights from their data.

One of Spark's great strengths is its efficiency in handling iterative algorithms and interactive data analysis. Since it keeps data in memory, iterative computations such as machine learning algorithms can run more smoothly and quickly. The ability to access and manipulate data in-memory reduces computation time significantly, making Spark an excellent choice for iterative processes.

Kafka

Kafka is a popular platform used for real-time data streaming and event processing. It's reliable and efficient, and a good choice for handling continuous data flows. With Kafka, organizations can easily publish, subscribe and process real-time data streams. This makes it perfect for creating dynamic and strong real-time data pipelines. It allows data to move smoothly from where it's produced to where it's used, allowing various applications and systems to work with the data in real time.

Kafka is designed to manage massive volumes of data without delay, making sure data is processed and sent to its destination fast. This is why it is well-suited for applications that need real-time updates and fast response times.

Kafka's distributed nature means it's reliable and can handle failures well. Data is replicated across multiple computers in a cluster, ensuring that, even if something goes wrong, the data remains safe and available. This makes Kafka a robust and trustworthy solution for important applications.

Azure HDInsight

Azure HDInsight is a service from Microsoft Azure designed to handle big data. It offers a smooth and easy experience for organizations that want to use big data in the cloud. With HDInsight, businesses can easily set up and manage different big data tools like Hadoop, Spark, HBase and Kafka, all on the Azure platform.

By using HDInsight, organizations get access to powerful tools that can process and analyse data on a large scale. HDInsight supports popular big data tools, making it compatible with many types of data tasks and analysis.

Cloud-based data warehousing

Cloud-based data warehousing offers a flexible and modern solution for storing and managing large data volumes in a public cloud environment. Data is stored in distributed and scalable systems, enabling organizations to adjust their storage needs based on demand without upfront hardware investments. The data is structured in a manner that simplifies querying and analysis, making use of powerful analytics tools.

A cloud data warehouse serves as an ideal choice for businesses that heavily rely on data and prioritize agility, flexibility and ease of use for their infrastructure needs. It provides quick access to data, facilitating efficient decision-making. With this approach, businesses can adapt to changing data requirements while benefiting from the convenience and capabilities offered by cloud technology. Here's a step-by-step overview of how it works:

- *Data storage:* Data is stored in a cloud-based storage system. This system often uses special ways of organizing the data that allow it to handle a lot of information and make sure it's safe. Cloud companies provide strong and safe storage options, allowing businesses to keep huge amounts of data securely.
- *Data ingestion:* Data comes from different places like databases, apps, devices and outside feeds and it's put into the cloud data warehouse. This is done using special tools, connections, or ways of talking to make sure the data moves smoothly into the warehouse.
- *Data structuring:* The data is then organized and set up in a particular way that makes it easy to query and analyse. This involves defining data schemas, partitioning and optimizing the data layout for faster access.
- *Data processing:* Cloud data warehouses can manage complex tasks involving data processing, transformation, aggregation

and computation. These tasks can be done using Structured Query Language (SQL)-like queries (a common language for databases), data pipelines (a way to move and transform data) or advanced tools for analysis.

- *Data analytics and insights:* Data analysts, data scientists and business users can perform advanced analytics and extract insights from the data stored in the cloud data warehouse. They can run complex queries, perform data visualization and use machine learning algorithms to uncover valuable information.

Benefits of a cloud-based data warehouse

A cloud data warehouse is a tool offering a range of advantages that cater to the evolving demands of modern data management. Some of the benefits of adopting a cloud data warehouse include:

- *Scalability:* A core strength of cloud data warehouses is their innate scalability, allowing seamless adjustment of storage and computational resources to varying data demands. This adaptability eliminates the need for significant upfront hardware investments, offering operational agility to handle unexpected spikes in data without disruption.
- *Cost efficiency:* Cloud data warehouses operate on a pay-as-you-go model, ensuring cost predictability by charging only for utilized resources. This relieves organizations from the financial burden of procuring and managing on-premises infrastructure, providing financial flexibility and budget optimization.
- *Performance enhancement:* Leveraging the distributed architecture of the cloud, data warehouses excel in rapid processing of complex queries and analytics tasks. This heightened performance translates to real-time or near-real-time insights, empowering informed decision-making.
- *Global accessibility:* Cloud data warehouses enable data access from anywhere with an internet connection, fostering seamless collaboration among geographically dispersed teams. This accessibility promotes unified access to shared

datasets, facilitating collaboration and innovation across organizational boundaries.

- *Advanced security and compliance:* Prominent cloud data warehouse providers prioritize security, implementing robust encryption, access controls and compliance adherence. This focus on security safeguards sensitive data and ensures compliance with industry regulations, which is crucial for businesses operating within regulated environments.
- *Managed services:* Cloud data warehouses often come with managed services, alleviating routine operational tasks such as data backups, updates and security patches. This managed approach allows internal IT teams to focus on deriving insights from the data.
- *Real-time analytics:* Many cloud data warehouses support real-time or near-real-time analytics, enabling swift responses to market trends, customer behaviour and emerging opportunities, providing a competitive edge.

Drawbacks of a cloud-based data warehouse

While cloud-based data warehouses provide the above benefits, they also have certain potential drawbacks that you should be aware of:

- *Costs:* Even though you only pay for what you use in the beginning, the total expenses for cloud-based data warehousing can become quite large as time goes on, particularly for organizations dealing with lots of data and complex processing needs. When you have more and more data, the monthly fees for storing it and using the computing power can go up, which means you end up spending more money.
- *Data transfer and latency:* Moving large amounts of data to and from the cloud can be time-consuming and may result in increased latency, especially if the organization's internet connection isn't very fast or stable. This can impact real-time data processing and analytics, leading to delays in decision-making.

- *Data security concerns:* Some organizations are hesitant to store sensitive or confidential data in the cloud because they worry about security and privacy. Even though cloud providers invest in strong security measures, organizations still need to trust external parties with their data. This can lead to concerns about keeping information confidential and complying with data privacy regulations.
- *Dependency on third parties:* Relying on a cloud provider for data warehousing services means you're dependent on their systems, how often they're available and how well they work. If the provider has a problem or their technology doesn't work correctly, it can cause a halt in accessing the data and affect what the organization does.

Data analytics and machine learning in the cloud

In this section, we will highlight how data analysis and machine learning in the cloud work together in various industries, discussing use cases that highlight the transformative impact of this technology combination.

There are so many industries that can use data analytics and machine learning in the cloud for business optimization. This technology combination empowers industries to innovate, adapt and thrive in the dynamic landscape of the digital age. Some of the industries that benefit are highlighted below.

Retail

In the retail sector, cloud-based data analytics and machine learning offer valuable solutions for improving customer experiences and optimizing operations. Retailers can analyse customer purchasing behaviour, preferences and historical data to create personalized marketing and recommendations. Inventory management also becomes more efficient by predicting demand, optimizing stock levels and reducing excess inventory. Real-time analytics can also help retailers monitor sales trends, understand the sentiment of their customers and adapt pricing strategies dynamically so that they can sell out faster.

Finance

In the finance industry, using the cloud for data analytics and machine learning is incredibly important, especially for detecting fraud, managing risks and making smart investment choices. Financial institutions really benefit from the cloud's ability to handle big tasks quickly and easily.

For example, spotting strange patterns in lots of transactions is crucial to stop fraud in its tracks. It can identify a problem before it causes more trouble and it helps keep both the bank and its customers safe and happy.

When it comes to deciding whether someone should get a loan, machine learning models play a big role. These models can analyse a wide range of data points, beyond what traditional methods could manage, resulting in more accurate credit risk evaluations. Lenders can make better-informed decisions about extending credit, optimizing their loan portfolios and minimizing default risks.

Also, having real-time market data accessible through the cloud is valuable for financial organizations. They can use this current data to create smart trading strategies, which allows them to react swiftly and precisely to market changes. This gives them a competitive advantage in their trading activities, helping them seize market opportunities and stand out from the competition.

Manufacturing

Using cloud-based analytics in manufacturing can really boost how things work efficiently. This is because it helps with predictive maintenance, quality control and making the supply chain work better.

Imagine a factory which uses machines to manufacture different products. With cloud-based analytics, they can monitor the health of the machines in real time. They can even anticipate periods when a machine might break down and fix it before it causes big problems. This helps the factory stay up and running most of the time.

Also, when it comes to quality control, cloud-based analytics can help a lot. They can find ways to make fewer mistakes and waste less material. This can lead to reduced defects, optimized allocation of resources and cost savings.

Cloud-based analytics can also optimize the supply chain. By using predictive analytics, manufacturers can predict demand patterns, effectively manage inventory levels and streamline logistics operations. This leads to two benefits: saving money by using resources more efficiently and seamless fulfilment of market demand.

Education

The fusion of cloud-based data analytics and machine learning has a profound impact on the educational landscape. They're making learning more personalized, improving how well students do in school and making school tasks easier.

Let's see how this works. With cloud-based data analytics and machine learning, schools can look at how students are doing and identify where they might need extra help. This means students can get the support they need to do better in school.

A lot of specialized schools, online-learning platforms and higher education institutions are leveraging data analytics to make the educational experience better.

REVIEW

As we conclude this chapter, it's clear that the integration of cloud-based data analytics and machine learning has the power to reshape industries, education and countless other aspects of our world. The possibilities for innovation and transformation are boundless and the journey is just beginning.

The cloud offers a limitless playground for big data to thrive, where its potential can be fully harnessed. If you're a student who is curious about the future of technology, an educator dedicated to shaping minds, a business leader seeking innovative solutions, or anyone intrigued by the evolving tech landscape, now is the perfect time to embrace these tools and unlock their potential. With the cloud as our canvas, we can bring data-driven insights to the forefront, and with the power of machine learning we can unlock new ways of understanding and prediction that were once unimaginable.

GLOSSARY

BUSINESS TRANSFORMATION: The use of big data to drive innovation and change within organizations, enabling more informed decision-making, uncovering new growth opportunities and enhancing competitive strategies.

DATA ANONYMIZATION: The process of securing private or sensitive information by deleting or encrypting the identifiers that link an individual to stored data.

DATA PRE-PROCESSING: The initial step in data analysis, involving cleaning, transforming and organizing data to ensure its quality and readiness for analysis.

PSEUDONYMIZATION: The process of deleting personal identifiers from data and replacing them with placeholder values.

VARIETY: One of big data's three Vs, it signifies the diverse types of data, including structured, semi-structured and unstructured formats like images and videos, making data integration and analysis more complex.

VELOCITY: One of big data's three Vs, it highlights the speed at which data is generated and needs to be processed. Real-time or near-real-time processing is essential to extract meaningful insights from rapidly accumulating data.

VISUALIZATION TECHNIQUES: Methods to represent data visually, such as graphs, charts and dashboards, to facilitate easier understanding of complex data patterns and relationships.

VOLUME: One of big data's three Vs, it pertains to the enormous quantity of data generated from various sources and activities, challenging traditional computing tools and methods.

## CHAPTER SIX

Virtual machines and containers in the cloud

Virtualization and containerization are fundamental concepts in cloud computing. Throughout this chapter, I want to take you on a journey that's a bit like how I learned these ideas – step by step, breaking down complex concepts into manageable pieces. This will serve as your guide, helping you see how these two concepts join forces to create something truly powerful. I've been there myself, trying to wrap my head around these concepts, so I know the importance of learning them in a clear and understandable way.

We'll start by uncovering the basics of virtualization and containerization – two methods that make technology more efficient. This chapter explains how using virtual machines and containers together can revolutionize the way businesses operate.

You'll also learn how virtualization makes one big computer act like many small ones, each doing its own thing. Containers, on the other hand, are like special boxes that hold apps and all their parts together, making them super portable.

From the basics, you'll be guided through real-world examples that highlight how virtual machines and containers improve resource management, make software development and deployment smoother and accelerate innovation. By the end of this chapter, you'll have a solid understanding of how virtual machines and containers in the cloud play a pivotal role in technology today.

Overview of virtualization and containerization

Virtualization is a foundational concept in modern computing, revolutionizing the way hardware resources are utilized and managed. At its core, virtualization is the process of creating a virtual version of a physical resource, such as a server, storage device or network, using software. It's like having lots of mini-computers inside one big computer. This technology enables a single physical resource to function as multiple virtual instances, each operating independently and efficiently.

The important thing that makes virtualization work is called the hypervisor. This is a software layer that sits between the real hardware and the virtual versions we create. The hypervisor acts like a bridge, separating and protecting the real resources. It's a guard that lets many virtual machines (VMs) run on one real computer. Each VM is like its own world, with its own operating system, programs and resources and they are completely isolated from other VMs on the same host.

Virtualization has many advantages. One of them is resource optimization, where a single physical server can be divided into multiple VMs, leading to better utilization of hardware. This way, we use the computer's abilities fully. Combining workloads like this helps to reduce costs, space and power consumption.

FIGURE 6.1   Virtualization vs containerization

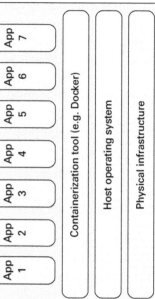

Virtualization

App 1	App 2	App 3
Binaries or libraries	Binaries or libraries	Binaries or libraries
Guest operating system	Guest operating system	Guest operating system

Hypervisor

Physical infrastructure

Containerization

App 1	App 2	App 3	App 4	App 5	App 6	App 7

Containerization tool (e.g. Docker)

Host operating system

Physical infrastructure

Additionally, virtualization enhances isolation and security, as each VM operates independently, preventing one VM from affecting others in case of issues.

Containerization, which shares some similarities with virtualization, uses a different kind of abstraction. It's a simpler form of virtualization that segregates applications and their requirements into self-contained bundles called containers. These containers are like independent boxes containing everything needed for an app to run, such as the app itself, libraries, runtime and settings. Unlike virtualization, where each virtual machine carries a whole operating system, containers share the host system's core, making them lighter and more effective.

In containerization, the core component is the container runtime and it is responsible for handling how the containers work. A very popular container runtime is Docker. Containers offer advantages such as portability, where an application packaged in a container can run consistently across different platforms and environments, from the software developer's laptop to a production server. Containers also start up quickly and use resources effectively due to their lightweight nature.

Container orchestration tools like Kubernetes have also taken containerization to the next level by enabling automated deployment, scaling and management of containerized applications. Kubernetes takes away the complexity of managing many containers at once, so developers and operations teams can pay more attention to creating and delivering applications.

Differences between virtualization and containerization

This section further breaks down the key differences between virtualization and containerization according to certain criteria.

- Abstraction level:
  - Virtualization operates at the hardware level, where it abstracts physical resources to generate virtual representations of servers, storage and networks. The management of these virtual machines is facilitated by a hypervisor.
  - Containerization operates at a higher level, where it abstracts the application and its dependencies into separate units called containers. These containers function independently, containing all the necessary components to execute the application.
- Resource utilization:
  - Virtual machines encapsulate complete operating systems, leading to higher resource overhead because of the need to manage multiple operating system instances on the same hardware.
  - Containers share the host OS kernel – this means that the resource overhead is significantly lower. This efficiency is from the fact that containers share all system resources, making them more lightweight.
- Deployment time:
  - Virtual machines have longer deployment times due to the need to start up an entire operating system for each instance.
  - Containers have faster deployment times as they require less overhead. They can be created and deployed almost instantaneously.
- Use cases:
  - Virtualization is suitable for scenarios that require strong isolation, legacy application support, testing environments and the management of diverse operating systems on a single server.
  - Containerization is very suitable for microservices architecture, DevOps practices and application scaling.

CASE STUDY   Containerization and virtualization in the music industry

I love music, so I will use it as an analogy for describing these technologies.

Containerization

To describe containerization, imagine a girl group called Dreamy Divas performing together. Dreamy Divas is like an application and each musician in the group is like a part of that application (libraries, code, settings and more). Now, imagine they are performing on a stage – that's the container. The stage keeps them organized and isolated from the audience (other applications), so they can perform all their songs without any interference. Just as each musician knows their part and plays it within the group's performance, each part of the application runs within its container.

Virtualization

To describe virtualization, think of a music festival with multiple musicians and stages. Each stage hosts a different musician, just like a virtual machine hosts a different operating system and applications. Each musician performs their own songs independently on their stage and they don't affect the other musicians. Similarly, each VM runs its own operating system and applications, isolated from other VMs on the same physical server. Just as the music from one stage doesn't mix with the music from another, the contents of one VM don't mix with the contents of another.

To wrap it up

Containerization is like organizing and isolating the musicians within a group on a single stage, while virtualization is like hosting multiple independent musicians on separate stages at a music festival. Both approaches offer different levels of isolation and resource management, helping applications run smoothly without interfering with each other.

Understanding virtual machines

A VM is a concept in modern computing that involves imitating an entire physical computer system within a software environment. This imitation encompasses virtualizing hardware parts such as the central processing unit (CPU), memory, storage and network connections. The main goal is to allow the running of various operating systems and applications simultaneously on just one physical host machine.

Every virtual machine consists of a specific collection of resources like processor cores, memory and storage capacity. These resources are taken from the pool available on the physical host. This allocation process is flexible, ensuring efficient use of resources and fair distribution among multiple VMs. The virtual hardware of the VM, which includes its CPU, memory and storage controllers, is presented to the guest operating system as if it were tangible, physical hardware.

The operating system of the VM, often known as the guest operating system, interacts with the virtual hardware elements supplied by the hypervisor. This separation between VMs guarantees that actions and modifications in one VM don't impact others. Additionally, it enables different operating systems to run concurrently, making it possible for diverse software environments and applications to smoothly coexist.

The advantages of virtual machines

There are multiple advantages of virtual machines in technology today. These advantages encompass a wide spectrum of enhancements that contribute significantly to the efficiency, flexibility and security of computing systems. Some of these advantages are listed below.

RESOURCE OPTIMIZATION

One of the prominent advantages for virtual machines is in resource optimization. By consolidating multiple virtual instances onto a single physical server, virtual machines enhance the effective allocation of hardware resources. This consolidation enables organizations to optimize processing power, memory, storage and network assets dynamically, responding to the demands of applications in real time. As a result, underutilization of resources is minimized, fostering a more efficient and sustainable use of physical hardware.

COST EFFICIENCY

Running VMs on one big computer can be very effective for modern businesses. Primarily, it helps put all the computer work in one place, which saves money. You don't need to buy and take care of many separate computers. This saves on things like buying the computers, the electricity they use, keeping them cool and the space they take up. And these savings extend beyond initial investments to encompass ongoing operational expenses as well. When you have fewer real computers, it's easier to take care of them. You can focus on optimizing performance, security protocols and software updates.

ACCELERATED SOFTWARE DEVELOPMENT AND TESTING

Virtual machines are important in software development and testing processes. They make it easy for developers to quickly set up isolated environments to test software updates, configurations and new applications. This significantly enhances the efficiency of development cycles and reduces the time it takes to bring new products to market because engineering teams can rapidly test software. Just like how prototypes help engineers refine their designs before mass production, virtual machines allow developers to fine-tune their software in controlled spaces before its official release. This not only accelerates the development process but also ensures that the final product is to a certain standard.

HARDWARE INDEPENDENCE

Virtual machines introduce a layer of abstraction that separates the software from the specifics of the underlying hardware. This abstraction is like a universal translator that enables the same VM image to seamlessly operate on various physical servers, regardless of their unique configurations. This remarkable attribute ensures that VMs are exceptionally portable and versatile. They can easily work on different types of computers without having problems with compatibility.

EDUCATION AND TRAINING

In education, virtual machines are widely used to help students gain hands-on experience and explore different operating systems, software and networking setups in a safe and controlled environment. This way of teaching allows students to try things out, learn from mistakes and understand concepts without worrying about causing problems in real systems or networks. With VMs, students can simulate real-life situations, try various technologies and develop practical skills that are important for their studies and future careers. Additionally, VMs make it easy for students to work together on projects by providing a consistent setup that they can share – I've seen this a lot in cloud engineering courses and how they set up codelabs for practice. This use of VMs in education has become a crucial part of modern teaching methods, improving the quality of technical education and helping students understand complex ideas better.

The disadvantages of virtual machines

Although there are a lot of advantages to virtual machines, they also come with their share of disadvantages, and understanding the two sides helps you make informed decisions about their implementation. Here are some key drawbacks to consider:

COMPLEX MANAGEMENT

Managing multiple virtual machines can be complex and requires expertise. As the number of virtual machines increases, tasks such as configuring resources, handling networking and ensuring compatibility can become complex. Handling resources for each virtual machine, like CPU, memory and storage allocation, needs careful planning to ensure good performance and avoid bottlenecks.

Networking also becomes more complicated when dealing with many virtual machines. Assigning Internet Protocol (IP) addresses, managing network traffic and ensuring proper connectivity can be challenging, especially with diverse applications and services across virtual machines.

SECURITY

While virtual machines offer isolation, it's crucial to understand that vulnerabilities in one virtual machine can potentially affect others that share the same host. This arises from the fact that multiple virtual machines share the underlying physical host and its hypervisor. If a security breach happens in one virtual machine, it might exploit vulnerabilities in the hypervisor or other parts, potentially leading to unauthorized access or data exposure.

LICENSING COSTS

It's important to consider that certain operating systems and software licences might pertain to virtual machines, which could introduce potential cost considerations that should be taken into account within your budget planning. Licensing models for specific software can vary and they might be based on factors like the number of virtual processors, the amount of memory allocated, or the total number of virtual machines deployed. This means that, as you scale up your virtual machine infrastructure, the associated licensing costs could also increase. It's essential to thoroughly understand the licensing agreements associated with the software you plan to use in your virtual environment to ensure compliance and avoid unexpected expenses. This way, you can make informed decisions and allocate resources appropriately while being aware of the broader financial implications.

Understanding containers

Imagine you're a fashion influencer curating a diverse collection of outfits for an upcoming photoshoot. Each outfit has its own unique style, accessories and footwear and you're aiming to capture different moods and themes in your photos. However, managing all these outfit combinations can be quite a challenge.

To stay organized, you decide to use dedicated boxes for each outfit combination. Each box contains everything needed for a complete look – clothes, accessories, shoes and even make-up. This way, when it's time for the photoshoot, you can effortlessly pick the right box and have all the elements ready to create the desired look.

In technology, these fashion boxes can be likened to containers. Each container encapsulates an application along with its essential components (e.g. code, libraries, runtime and configurations). Just as each box is a self-contained unit for a complete outfit, containers provide a self-contained environment for applications to run smoothly.

Containers offer an efficient way to manage applications, much like how fashion boxes simplify outfit coordination. You can create, package and deploy applications within dedicated containers, ensuring consistent performance across various cloud environments. If an issue arises with one container, it doesn't affect others, similar to how a problem with one fashion box doesn't impact the others.

The beauty of containers lies in their ability to simplify complex applications and various setups. Just as fashion boxes make it easier to coordinate different outfits, containers empower developers to design and launch different applications seamlessly, regardless of the underlying infrastructure. This simplicity, combined with resource efficiency and rapid deployment, makes containers an important technology in cloud computing today.

How containers work

The container management process plays a pivotal role in the efficient deployment and operation of containerized applications. This process encompasses four distinct stages that guide the life cycle of applications and the services they encapsulate:

- *Creation:* The process of container management starts with the creation of container images. Developers bundle their application code, runtime environment, libraries, configurations and necessary dependencies into a singular container image. This image acts as a self-contained unit that encompasses all elements essential for the application's execution. This stage ensures that all components required for the application's operation are included in a standardized format.
- *Deployment:* After the creation of the container image, it is deployed onto the target infrastructure. This involves launching instances of the container image on specified host machines. The deployment process benefits from the consistency and portability of containers, as the same container image can be deployed across various environments, from development to production.
- *Scaling:* With containers, you can scale depending on your application workloads. When application demand increases, multiple instances of the same container can be launched simultaneously to handle the load. Container orchestration platforms like Kubernetes help to manage and scale containers automatically.

- *Destruction:* As applications progress through their life cycle, there might be a need to decommission containers. The destruction stage involves stopping and removing container instances that are no longer needed. This ensures that there is no unnecessary usage of computing resources.

The advantages of containers

Like virtual machines, containers have many advantages. These benefits are the reason for their widespread adoption and growing popularity in the world of technology. Some of the advantages are as follows.

MICROSERVICES
Containers play a fundamental role in the microservices architecture, which allows developers to build applications as a set of small, self-contained services that can be deployed separately. This method of designing applications in smaller pieces brings several advantages, such as improved flexibility, ease of maintaining each part separately and the ability to update specific components without affecting the whole application. This way, developers can work on different parts of the application independently, making the development process more efficient and adaptable.

PORTABILITY
Containers are very portable and they allow applications to run consistently across different platforms and environments. Developers can put everything an app needs into a container image, which makes it simple to move apps between cloud providers, on-premises servers and developer workstations.

RESOURCE OPTIMIZATION
Using tools like Kubernetes, containers can be managed and scaled automatically as needed. This efficient use of resources aids resource optimization, cuts down on expenses and promotes sustainable infrastructure management.

SCALING

Containers make it easy to scale horizontally by allowing applications to be replicated across multiple containers. This flexibility lets apps deal with different amounts of users and requests, ensuring they work well without over provisioning resources.

The disadvantages of containers

Containers offer remarkable benefits such as enhanced portability, streamlined deployment and efficient resource utilization. However, like any technology, they come with their set of challenges that need careful consideration.

NETWORKING

Networking containers, especially across different hosts or settings, can be very challenging. Container networking involves creating connections between containers and external services, which demands meticulous planning and management. It's essential to set up the right configurations to ensure smooth communication among containers and with other services outside the container environment. This can be a technically demanding task that requires careful attention and expertise.

COMPLEXITY

Managing containers can be complex, especially in large-scale environments. Container orchestration tools like Kubernetes aim to simplify this, but they can also introduce their own complexities.

STORAGE

Containers are designed to be stateless, meaning that containers don't have the ability to store data or state. This can complicate the handling of data that needs to be kept over time, like databases, in a container setup. Nonetheless, there are solutions like 'persistent volumes' that can be used to manage and safeguard data within a Docker container.

Container orchestration with Kubernetes

Before we start talking about Kubernetes and how it works its magic, let's first define what container orchestration means. In music, orchestration can be defined as the arrangement of different instruments to create a harmonious composition. Each instrument has its own part to play, contributing to the overall sound and rhythm of the song.

With containers, orchestration follows a similar principle. Just as a musical conductor coordinates the various instruments to create a cohesive performance, container orchestration involves managing and coordinating multiple containers to create a cohesive application performance. With container orchestration, ensuring applications work seamlessly includes tasks like deploying containers, scaling them based on demand, managing their network communication and recovering them if they fail.

In container orchestration, Kubernetes takes on a role similar to the conductor in music orchestration – managing the containerized applications. Kubernetes orchestrates containers to create a harmonious environment for applications to thrive by automating the deployment, scaling and management of containerized applications.

What are containerized applications?

Containerized applications are software applications that are packaged along with all their dependencies, configurations and runtime environments into boxes called containers. These containers typically provide an isolated environment for the application to run on.

Containerized applications have a strong connection with the idea of microservices. Microservices is a way of designing applications where they're split into smaller, separate services that can be developed, deployed and managed independently. These individual services each have a specific responsibility and communicate with other services through API calls.

You can use containers to implement the microservices architecture. Each microservice can be enclosed within its own container. This isolation lets various microservices have their unique runtime environments and requirements, which reduces the chance of issues between services.

IS THERE ANOTHER ARCHITECTURE BEYOND MICROSERVICES?

Yes. There's also the monolith architecture and this has been around longer than microservices. With monoliths, applications are built as a single, interconnected unit. All logic and functionalities are tightly integrated and they interact directly with each other.

Monoliths make software development and deployment straightforward. Since the entire application is in one codebase, software developers can work on different features without needing to manage multiple services. Monoliths also simplify debugging since there's a single point of reference for issues.

However, monoliths can become difficult to manage as the application grows in complexity and scale. Changing the implementation of one function or module can affect another part of the code, leading to unexpected bugs and errors. Scaling a monolithic application can also be challenging, because it involves scaling the entire application rather than specific components.

The major difference between monoliths and microservices lies in their architectural approach. Monoliths create applications as single unified units, while microservices break them into smaller, independently deployable services that communicate via APIs. Monoliths offer simplicity but can become cumbersome as applications scale, while microservices prioritize flexibility and scalability.

FIGURE 6.2 Monoliths vs microservices

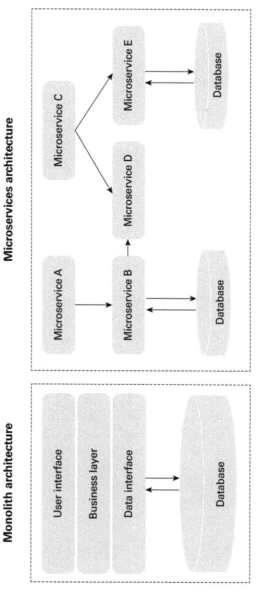

Monolith architecture

Microservices architecture

Now that you've learned about containerized applications and where containers are largely used, it's time to see how Kubernetes works its magic.

Overview of a Kubernetes cluster

A Kubernetes cluster is a collection of interconnected computers, or nodes, that work together to manage and run containerized applications.

Within the cluster, there are different concepts that Kubernetes uses to manage applications effectively. These concepts include:

- *Pod:* A Kubernetes Pod is a collection of one or more containers sharing the same network and storage resources and is the smallest deployable unit of a Kubernetes application.
- *Service:* A Service is an abstraction layer that provides network connectivity and load balancing for Pods or other services within the cluster.
- *ReplicaSet:* A ReplicaSet is a Kubernetes object that ensures that a specified number of Pod replicas are running at all times, facilitating high availability and scaling.
- *Deployment:* A Kubernetes deployment provides instructions to Kubernetes on creating or modifying instances of Pods that hold containerized applications. Deployments aid in effectively scaling the number of replica Pods, facilitating the rollout of updated code and rolling back to a previous deployment version if needed.
- *ConfigMap:* A ConfigMap is an API object enabling the storage of data in the form of key-value pairs.
- *Secret:* A Secret is an object that contains sensitive data like tokens or passwords.
- *Namespace:* A Namespace provides a way to divide cluster resources among multiple users, teams, or projects.

- *Ingress:* An Ingress is an object that manages external access to the services within the cluster. It serves as an entry point or gateway for external traffic to reach services running within the cluster.
- *Volume:* A Volume in Kubernetes is a directory with data that can be accessed across multiple containers in a Pod.

The Kubernetes cluster has something called a Control Plane at its core. It is also referred to as the master Kubernetes node. This Control Plane is responsible for managing and coordinating the cluster's activities. It consists of the following key components:

- *API Server:* The API Server is the central communication hub in a Kubernetes cluster. It receives and processes commands and requests from users and various components. The API Servers makes interaction between human users, applications and the Kubernetes environment seamless.
- *Controller Manager:* The Controller Manager maintains the alignment between the desired state and the actual state of the cluster. This component monitors resources and keeps track of what is happening in the Kubernetes cluster to ensure that applications and services behave as intended.
- *Scheduler:* The Scheduler ensures Pod placement by assigning Pods to Nodes. It determines which Nodes are accurate placements for each Pod in the scheduling queue based on resource availability and constraints.
- *etcd:* This is a consistent and highly available key-value storage that holds all the configuration data and state of the cluster.

Beyond the master node, there are other nodes within the cluster called worker nodes and these nodes host the actual containerized applications. The worker nodes consist of two key components:

- *Kubelet:* The Kubelet is the primary 'Node Agent' that runs on each node. It communicates with the Control Plane and ensures that containers are running in a Pod.

FIGURE 6.3   Kubernetes architecture

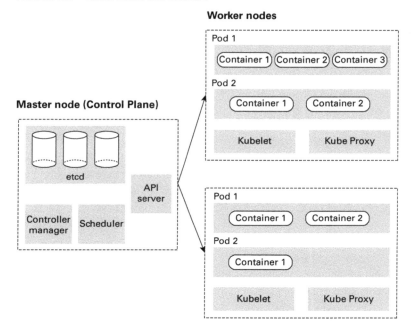

- *Kube Proxy:* Kube Proxy is a network proxy on every node within the cluster, responsible for executing a part of the Kubernetes Service concept. It maintains network rules that allow network communication to and from Pods.

A CULINARY EXPLORATION OF KUBERNETES

Let's imagine that you own a small-scale food business and have received a huge investment to scale your business. You've now rebranded your restaurant to KubeBistro and you get thousands of orders daily. To keep things organized in your kitchen, you have created a special system in your restaurant.

You've hired a head chef who manages everything in the restaurant including the menus, orders, inventory and cooking stations. This chef is like the Control Plane in Kubernetes, overseeing everything happening in the restaurant. When customers come into the restaurant, they go to the counter to place their food order. From the counter, the food order is taken and processed. This counter is like the API Server where commands are received and processed.

KubeBistro serves only three-course meals and each meal consists of different types of courses. In KubeBistro, a Pod is like a complete three-course meal (or dish) with everything needed to serve – the starter, main course and dessert. Each course is comprised of different things. For example, banana bread contains bananas, sugar, eggs and flour, and these different ingredients play their unique roles in the taste and output of the food. In KubeBistro, these components (or ingredients) are like containers, individual units with specific roles that come together to create the complete dish.

In the KubeBistro kitchen, there are different stations for cooking. Some stations are for grilling, while others are for frying or baking. Nodes are like these stations where Pods are placed to be cooked. Each Node has its own set of tools and resources. Throughout the cooking, to maintain consistency in the taste regardless of who cooks, you create recipe cards for different chefs to use as references. These recipe cards are like ConfigMaps, because they hold the settings and 'configurations' for the different meals.

Once the order is ready to be served to the customer, the server brings dishes from the kitchen to the table. In KubeBistro, Services guide the flow of traffic to the right Pods, making sure each three-course meal (Pod) reaches the right table (customer/user). For subsequent orders that are similar to previous orders, you might need to prepare more of the same dish. ReplicaSets ensure you have the right number of identical dishes ready to serve, even if some are eaten or spoiled.

The section above used a restaurant metaphor to explain Kubernetes. Now replace everything about cooking with the Kubernetes concepts you've learned earlier and I hope it's clear. Just as in the kitchen scenario, Kubernetes coordinates and manages the various elements of your applications to ensure they function seamlessly together. Each analogy translates to a specific Kubernetes component or concept, giving you a practical way to understand how this powerful technology works. So, the next time you think about orchestrating applications and managing containerized workloads, you can draw upon the familiar image of your expertly run restaurant kitchen to help you navigate Kubernetes harmoniously.

REVIEW

In this chapter, you learned about containerization and virtualization, and the difference between these two technologies. I hope that you now have a solid grasp of their fundamentals and unique features and you're able to make informed decisions when it comes to selecting the right technology for your specific needs. Additionally, you gained insights into some of the fundamental concepts of Kubernetes, a powerful container orchestration platform that plays a vital role in modern application deployment and management.

Containers and virtual machines are very important technologies in cloud engineering and you will see them being used extensively in different industries that leverage technology. These technologies help in shaping the modern computing landscape by providing innovative solutions to challenges related to resource utilization, scalability and application deployment. With Kubernetes, you also have an idea of advanced container orchestration, understanding how it empowers applications to perform seamlessly in dynamic environments. This knowledge equips you to navigate cloud technologies and contribute to the efficient operation of digital initiatives you come across.

GLOSSARY

CONTAINER IMAGE: A container image is a lightweight, standalone and executable software package that includes everything needed to run a piece of software, including code, runtime, libraries and settings.

CONTAINER RUNTIME: The component that aids managing and executing containers. Docker is a popular container runtime that handles the creation, deployment and operation of containers.

CONTROL PLANE: The Control Plane is the core management component of a Kubernetes cluster. It consists of the API server, controller manager, scheduler and etcd, collectively responsible for orchestrating and managing the cluster's operations.

HIGH AVAILABILITY (HA): High availability is a design principle focused on ensuring that applications remain accessible and operational even in the face of hardware failures or other disruptions.

HORIZONTAL SCALING: Horizontal scaling involves adding or removing instances of an application (containers or Pods) to handle changes in load.

HYPERVISOR: A special software layer that sits between the physical hardware and the virtual instances created through virtualization. It separates and protects the real resources, allowing multiple VMs to run on one physical computer.

LOAD BALANCING: Load balancing is the distribution of network traffic across multiple servers or containers to prevent overloading of a single resource.

NETWORK PROXY: A network proxy is a server or software that acts as an intermediary for requests from clients seeking resources from other servers or services.

NODE AGENT: A Node Agent is a software component that runs on each node in a Kubernetes cluster. It communicates with the Control Plane and ensures containers within the node are properly managed and functioning.

RESOURCE ISOLATION: Resource isolation is the practice of segregating and protecting computing resources to prevent one application or container from impacting others. Both virtualization and containerization provide resource isolation to enhance security and stability.

RESOURCE UTILIZATION: Resource utilization measures how efficiently hardware resources like CPU, memory and storage are utilized by applications.

## CHAPTER SEVEN

Cloud engineering and DevOps

This is my favourite chapter in this book and that's because I get to share about continuous integration and continuous deployment (CI/CD), infrastructure automation and some elements of the cloud that I frequently teach. In this chapter, I will take you through cloud engineering and DevOps step by step so that you will be confident about these concepts by the chapter's end. We'll start by exploring cloud engineering and DevOps principles. These intertwined practices have changed the way we do software development, enabling teams to deliver applications with remarkable speed and efficiency.

We'll cover CI/CD, infrastructure as code (IaC) and also shed light on the crucial domains of monitoring, logging and performance optimization. As we embark on this journey through cloud engineering and DevOps, you're in for a treat of technical insight and practical wisdom.

Introduction to cloud engineering

Cloud engineering is the strategy of applying engineering principles into cloud computing. This means leveraging techniques and best practices from the field of engineering to design, create and manage cloud-based systems. It involves using techniques to ensure that cloud resources are used efficiently, applications run smoothly and data is secure. By integrating engineering principles with cloud technology, cloud engineering optimizes performance, scalability and reliability in technology.

In this scenario, picture yourself as someone who owns a make-up store that's getting increasingly popular. At first, you had everything in one small shop. But as more customers come in, things start to slow down. Sometimes, the store gets so crowded that it's hard for people to buy what they want.

You're thinking about the longevity of your business and you decide to build an online store for make-up that is available to all your global customers. This is where cloud engineering comes into play. You decide to transition your business to an online business using cloud-based infrastructure. Instead of relying on physical sales, you distribute your application across multiple virtual servers in the cloud. Cloud engineering guides you in designing a scalable architecture where resources can be added or removed based on demand. During normal days, your application uses just enough resources to keep things running smoothly as orders come in. However, when Black Friday arrives and the traffic spikes, your cloud setup automatically scales up, allocating more computing power and bandwidth to handle the increased load.

Cloud engineering also enables you to enhance your website's reliability, which is great for your make-up business. You set up automated backups and redundancy across different cloud regions. If one region experiences issues, your traffic is seamlessly redirected to another, minimizing downtime. Plus, you utilize cloud-based databases to ensure your customer data is secure and accessible from anywhere.

As a result of applying cloud engineering principles, your business not only delivers a seamless shopping experience during high-demand periods but also grows sustainably as your business expands. By strategically leveraging the capabilities of the cloud, you've engineered a system that is flexible, reliable and responsive to the dynamic needs of your business and customers.

Cloud engineering is revolutionizing different industries. From finance to entertainment and even governments, it has created opportunities for software development teams to innovate, collaborate and streamline their processes. It's exciting to see how teams across the world are constantly evolving their methods and delivering better products and services to users globally.

The financial services sector has greatly evolved as a result of cloud engineering principles. I'm not too old (yet), but I remember when banking was a lot harder to do. Traditional banking models have given way to agile, customer-centric approaches which allow us to withdraw, deposit, transfer and review our finances with ease and this is as a result of different technologies, including the cloud. Cloud-powered platforms facilitate real-time transactions, personalized wealth management and risk assessment. Software development teams, infused with the possibilities of the cloud, are creating interesting fintech solutions that democratize financial services, bridge gaps and redefine how we manage and interact with money.

The entertainment industry has embraced cloud engineering to revolutionize how content is made, distributed and enjoyed. With the help of cloud-based teamwork tools, developers, designers and creators collaborate seamlessly, speeding up content creation and refining the whole process. One big plus is scalability – when movies, games or live streaming events hit the scene, the cloud quickly provides more power to keep things smooth. Streaming services rely on cloud storage and content delivery networks to make sure people worldwide can access content right away and without hiccups.

Cloud engineering is also the magic behind cloud gaming, where graphically demanding games can be played on simple devices, thanks to some remote magic. Data-driven insights obtained from user behaviour patterns in the cloud also drive personalized content recommendations, making everyone more engaged.

Governments have also embraced cloud engineering to modernize and optimize their operations. Cloud engineering facilitates the digitization of citizen services in some countries, allowing people to interact with government agencies online, reducing paperwork and wait times. By harnessing cloud-based analytics and data storage, governments gain valuable insights from vast datasets, enabling informed decision-making and policy formulation. Additionally, the cloud enhances cyber security measures, safeguarding sensitive government data and ensuring compliance with strict security standards.

CASE STUDY   How is cloud engineering aiding innovation?

Cloud engineering is driving technology innovation. It's helping people collaborate, invent new products and services and make existing processes easier. It's like a toolbox filled with digital tools that innovators and creators can use to bring their ideas to life. With the cloud, innovators can quickly test out new concepts without worrying about setting up complex machines.

Scalability is one of the amazing features of cloud engineering. It enables innovations to grow as needed. Imagine starting with a little idea and growing it with the aid of the cloud into something substantial that many people may use. This eliminates the concern that innovators would run out of resources or space.

Cloud engineering helps businesses by enabling them to create and distribute innovative apps and services. They can use already-existing technologies on the cloud, which saves time and effort. Since innovators no longer need to start from scratch each time they want to create something new, technology innovation is sped up and made more accessible as a result.

Effectiveness, dependability and creativity are orchestrated in cloud engineering by automation. The impact of automation is extensive. It enables cloud engineers to provision resources, deploy apps and manage configurations using code-driven approaches. This not only ensures precision but also eliminates the possibility of human error. As automation takes over regular jobs, human efforts can be diverted toward more strategic and creative endeavours, fostering creativity and problem-solving.

In the next section we explore DevOps, a philosophy that integrates development and operations. DevOps increases collaboration and communication across traditionally siloed teams, much as automation optimizes cloud procedures. Together, they transform how software is produced, tested and delivered, all while adhering to the automation principles that enable cloud engineering.

DevOps principles and practices

DevOps is a philosophy that embraces agility, collaboration and automation. It is a set of methods, values and collaborative approaches that bring together software development (Dev) and IT operations (Ops) teams to accelerate and improve the entire software delivery life cycle. DevOps' fundamental objective is to integrate and automate processes so that businesses can create, test, release and manage software products more quickly and more effectively.

As a result of the DevOps culture, software engineering teams now work in harmony to create, deploy and refine applications with unprecedented efficiency and speed. The traditional barriers between development and operations have dissolved, giving rise to seamless collaboration and a shared sense of responsibility.

Software development and operations were frequently viewed as separate and independent entities prior to the widespread adoption of DevOps. With little inter-team communication and collaboration, these teams worked independently. The software development life cycle was impacted by a number of issues and inefficiencies as a result of this separation.

The majority of the time, developers would focus on writing code and adding new features without considering the potential operational challenges associated with deploying and maintaining their product in practical settings. After development was finished, the code would be given to the operations team for deployment, which could result in delays, misalignments and even mistakes because different environments have different configurations.

Additionally, this conventional method led to lengthier release cycles and slower response times to changes and user input. Frequent manual interventions, such as establishing environments and setting up servers, were time-consuming and prone to error.

Pre-DevOps wasn't a good time to build large-scale applications with ease. But now, thanks to advanced DevOps principles, creating and managing such applications has become a whole new ball game.

Five major principles of DevOps

For over a decade, DevOps has been evolving. And it has evolved over time across different organizations. This evolution has led to the emergence of different flavours or approaches to DevOps, each tailored to suit specific contexts and objectives. Regardless of the flavour of DevOps you find, you'd see these five principles at play at the core of the entire system:

- *Collaboration:* DevOps is centred on collaboration. It involves eliminating traditional barriers between development, operations and other relevant teams within an organization. These teams can share knowledge, objectives and responsibilities when they collaborate closely, creating a more effective work environment. Collaboration ensures that everyone is on the same page and working toward the same goals. Additionally, it promotes a sense of shared ownership in which successes and setbacks are shared experiences.

- *Automation:* Automation is another fundamental pillar of DevOps. Throughout the software development and delivery life cycle, repetitive and manual operations are automated utilizing tools and scripts. By automating tasks like code testing, deployment and infrastructure provisioning, organizations reduce human error, enhance efficiency and accelerate processes. Automation makes workflows consistent, repeatable and less susceptible to errors, which eventually results in quicker and more dependable software releases.

- *CI/CD:* Continuous integration involves developers frequently integrating their code changes into a shared repository. Automated tests are executed to catch issues early in the development process, ensuring that new code integrates smoothly with the existing codebase. By automating the deployment of code changes to diverse environments, continuous delivery expands on continuous integration and makes software deployable at any time. Organizations are able to release new features and upgrades quickly, consistently and with little risk thanks to CI/CD.

- *Continuous improvement and learning:* Teams regularly seek feedback through observation, testing and user interactions to pinpoint areas that should be improved. By prioritizing improvements that are in line with user wants and market demands, this feedback-driven strategy aids companies in making wise decisions. Software solutions adapt and remain competitive in a continuously changing environment thanks to continuous learning and enhancement.

- *Shorter feedback loops:* Feedback loops shorten the interval between making a change and learning about its effects. Teams can identify and resolve problems more rapidly because

FIGURE 7.1   The DevOps life cycle

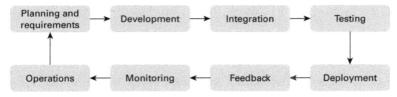

of shorter feedback loops, which enhances the overall quality of the software and user happiness. By gathering insights from real-world environments and user interactions, organizations can make data-driven decisions and respond swiftly to new possibilities and challenges.

These five principles together create a foundation for DevOps practices that promote more automation, agility and the delivery of high-quality software solutions. They promote a culture of continuous improvement and learning, where teams collaborate to meet changing business needs and exceed customer expectations.

The DevOps life cycle incorporates the principles of DevOps smoothly, making them a crucial component of how software is envisioned, created, delivered and maintained. When correctly implemented, these principles serve as a roadmap for and source of information for each stage of the software delivery process, supporting an all-encompassing strategy that prioritizes collaboration, automation, continuous integration and delivery, continuous improvement and short feedback loops.

Continuous integration and continuous deployment (CI/CD)

Continuous integration is the process whereby different software engineers merge code changes into the application's repository on a regular basis. After merging, the procedure conducts automated builds and tests to ensure that the new code is correct.

Continuous integration is crucial in modern app development for different reasons. It reduces the occurrence of bugs by allowing developers to test code in smaller portions, minimizing the risk of undetected issues in production. Continuous integration also streamlines code integration, enabling efficient creation and merging of pull requests. This benefit is valuable when development teams work on different features across various branches, as continuous integration tools help resolve code conflicts. Continuous integration also facilitates automated testing, making it simpler for developers to create and manage testing plans and scripts. This saves time for testers and the testing process can evolve within the CI pipeline. Additionally, continuous integration ensures the compatibility of libraries and checks for vulnerabilities in third-party dependencies, enhancing overall software security and reliability.

Typically, CI encompasses these key stages:

- *Code changes and pull requests:* A developer creates and pushes code changes from their local branch to the central repository's development branch. Subsequently, they initiate a pull request to merge the development branch into the main branch.
- *Code review:* An experienced team member evaluates the code submitted in the development branch and either endorses or declines the pull request. If declined, the reviewer usually provides specific feedback.
- *Build:* Upon approval, an automated code-building process commences, generating artifacts from the new code.
- *Testing:* The built code artifacts undergo a series of automated tests.
- *Merge:* If the code build is successful, the code in the development branch merges into the main branch.

Continuous deployment represents an automated software release procedure that extends from the continuous integration process. The outcome of a successful continuous integration phase serves as the input for continuous deployment.

FIGURE 7.2   Continuous delivery vs continuous deployment

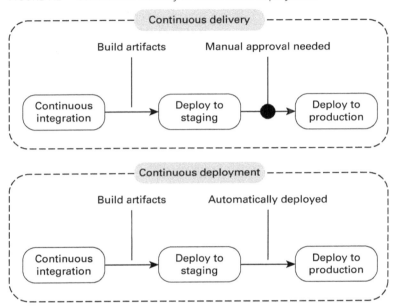

Beyond continuous deployment, there's also another 'CD' called continuous delivery. Continuous delivery is a method of automating code releases into production environments that require manual approval from a member of the software development team.

Continuous delivery first deploys artifacts created from source code in a test environment. After the automated tests in the CD pipeline are completed, quality assurance (QA) engineers do manual testing. Production deployment is approved once all tests and validation checks have been completed.

The difference between continuous delivery and continuous deployment is that continuous delivery involves manual testing and explicit approval before deployment, whereas continuous deployment automates the entire process.

Typically, CD consists of five processes:

- *Pre-production deployment:* The CI-build artifacts are deployed in this step to a pre-production (staging) environment.
- *Pre-production tests:* Automated tests are done on the pre-production environment at this phase to establish whether the application is functioning as intended. Checks for compliance and security flaws are among the other ones.
- *Production deployment:* The CD pipeline deploys code into the production environment when pre-production testing is successful.
- *Production tests:* After deploying the application to the production environment, the CD pipeline checks the application. Production testing is sometimes considered an optional phase; however, it should always be carried out, because pre-production environments may not have identified some issues due to variations in infrastructure, configuration settings, etc.
- *Monitor and feedback:* The application's stability and health are continuously monitored as part of this process and user input is also gathered. This feedback will serve as the foundation for the subsequent development cycle iteration.

THE ROLE OF CI/CD IN SOFTWARE DEVELOPMENT

In software development, continuous integration and continuous deployment play a crucial role in driving effectiveness, cooperation and dependability. An in-depth analysis of their functions is provided below:

- *Enhanced code management:* CI/CD allows multiple teams to work concurrently from a shared codebase using Git branches. The code repository and CI tools manage each team's contributions, offering a clear view of ongoing tasks and their statuses. Technical leads and reviewers can easily access the Git repository to monitor current branches, track code update timestamps, compare branch code with the main branch and review past CI pipeline runs for potential errors.

FIGURE 7.3   Steps in the continuous deployment process

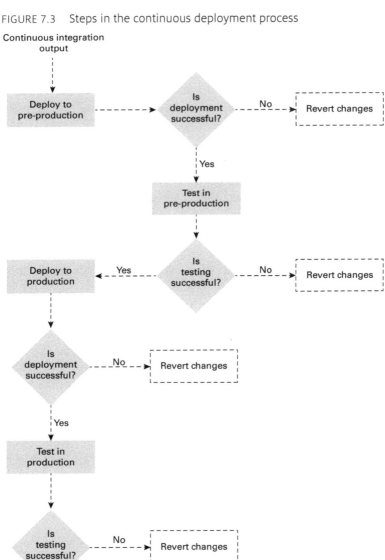

- *Effortless rollbacks:* The majority of CI/CD pipelines are created and structured to gracefully rollback in the event of a failure during code integration or deployment, restoring the source code repository (for CI) or the target environment (for CD) to their original conditions.
- *Automation benefits:* The overall code standard is improved through the use of automation technologies in CI to ensure that the checked-in code follows established coding standards. Functional and integration testing are largely automated by both CI and CD across several environments, giving test teams more time to do other in-depth checks. CI/CD reduces the risks associated with handling manual code by automating builds, tests and releases.
- *Conflict resolution:* When checking in code, software engineers risked overwriting each other's work with large bang deployments. Step-wise deployments, a technique used by CI/CD pipelines to reduce siloed development and remove code conflicts, reduce this risk.

To incorporate CI/CD into your application development process, you need to implement a CI/CD pipeline. A CI/CD pipeline is a software-based procedure that automates the integration of software source code and the deployment of applications. It closely resembles the CI and CD methods that we discussed.

You can trigger the CI/CD pipeline in a variety of ways. Some development teams decide to start a pipeline as soon as a pull request is approved and the code is merged into the main branch. Others create pipelines that run on the development branch as soon as the pull request is opened.

A SAMPLE CONTINUOUS INTEGRATION/CONTINUOUS DEPLOYMENT PIPELINE

trigger:
- main # Define the branch that triggers the pipeline when changes are pushed

---

```
pool:
vmImage: 'ubuntu-latest' # Specify the agent pool and image
to use

stages:
- stage: Build
jobs:
- job: BuildJob
 displayName: 'Build and Test'
 steps:
 - script: |
 # Install Node.js and npm
 curl -sL https://deb.nodesource.com/setup_14.x | sudo -E
bash -
 sudo apt-get install -y nodejs

 # Install project dependencies
 npm install

 # Build the application
 npm run build

 # Run tests
 npm test
 displayName: 'Build and Test'

 - publish: $(Build.ArtifactStagingDirectory)
 artifact: drop
 displayName: 'Publish Artifact'

- stage: DeployToStaging
jobs:
- job: DeployJob
 displayName: 'Deploy to Staging'
 steps:
 - download: current
 artifact: drop
```

```
- script: |
  echo "Deploying to staging..."
  displayName: 'Deploy to Staging'
```

The code snippet above is a sample CI/CD pipeline in YAML for Azure DevOps that builds, tests and deploys a JavaScript application. Let's go over what this pipeline is actually doing, line by line:

- *Trigger:* It specifies the branch that triggers the pipeline run. The pipeline is triggered when changes are pushed to the main branch.
- *Agent Pool:* It specifies the type of agent (virtual machine image) to use for running the pipeline. In this case, it's an Ubuntu-based agent.
- *Stages:* The pipeline consists of two stages: Build and DeployToStaging.
- *Build stage:*
  - The Build stage includes a job named BuildJob.
  - In the job, there are two steps:
    - The first step installs Node.js and npm, installs project dependencies, builds the application and runs tests.
    - The second step publishes the build artifacts to the Azure DevOps pipeline.
- *DeployToStaging stage:*
  - The DeployToStaging stage includes a job named Deploy-Job.
  - In the job, there are two steps:
    - The first step downloads the artifacts from the Build stage.
    - The second step echoes 'Deploying to staging...' in the console.

Infrastructure as code

The concept of IaC is also crucial in current software development and cloud computing. It is a method of managing and providing infrastructure that relies on code and automation rather than manual processes. Because of its numerous benefits, this technique has acquired widespread acceptance and now plays an important part in the DevOps and cloud engineering scene.

Prior to infrastructure as code, software development teams manually configured application infrastructure. To use this technique, you would need to go to the cloud provider's website, select the resources you want to create, follow the configuration steps and then complete your setup. To reprovision the infrastructure for a similar environment, you must follow the same methods.

Manual infrastructure configuration has various disadvantages in modern software development and cloud engineering. For a start, it is highly vulnerable to human error, which can result in misconfigurations, security vulnerabilities and system failures. Manual configurations also take time and are slow, limiting the agility required for rapid development and deployment. It also lacks version control and documentation, meaning that there is difficulty when it comes to tracking changes, effectively cooperating and troubleshooting issues.

IaC greatly improves deployments by offering numerous advantages. It automates the setup and configuration of infrastructure resources, reducing errors and ensuring uniformity. This automation accelerates deployment, resulting in quicker releases. IaC also utilizes version control, enabling teams to monitor changes, collaborate effectively and return to prior configurations when issues arise. It also supports scalability, allowing for dynamic resource allocation to manage varying workloads. IaC simplifies security and compliance by enabling the codification of security policies, guaranteeing consistent adherence to best practices. IaC functions as infrastructure documentation, aiding team members in comprehending, maintaining and troubleshooting configurations.

INFRASTRUCTURE AS CODE TOOLS

- *Terraform* is an IaC tool developed by HashiCorp. It serves as an orchestration and provisioning tool that empowers users to define and manage infrastructure resources across various cloud providers and on-premises environments. Terraform utilizes HashiCorp Configuration Language (HCL) or JSON for defining infrastructure configurations.

- *AWS CloudFormation* is AWS's dedicated IaC tool. It provides a native solution for defining and deploying AWS resources using JSON or YAML templates. CloudFormation is deeply integrated with AWS services, offering a comprehensive set of capabilities for managing AWS infrastructure. CloudFormation's notable strength is its tight coupling with AWS, allowing users to manage a wide range of AWS resources. It offers built-in support for AWS-specific services and advanced features like change sets for previewing updates. AWS CloudFormation is particularly well suited to AWS-centric environments.

- *Azure Bicep* is designed specifically for Microsoft Azure and serves as an abstraction layer for Azure Resource Manager (ARM) templates. It introduces the Bicep language, which simplifies the authoring of ARM templates, making them more human-readable and maintainable. Azure Bicep's primary strength lies in its enhanced readability and reduced complexity compared to raw ARM templates. It leverages native Azure support and allows users to define Azure infrastructure as code efficiently. It aligns closely with Microsoft Azure's offerings and is particularly suitable for Azure-focused environments.

- *Google Cloud Deployment Manager* is Google Cloud's IaC tool, enabling users to define and deploy resources within the GCP ecosystem. It supports YAML or Jinja2 templates for resource definitions and deployments. Deployment Manager's strength lies in its native integration with GCP, making it a seamless choice for managing GCP resources. It offers templating capabilities, facilitating resource management and automation within Google Cloud environments.

- *OpenStack Heat* is tailored for OpenStack, an open-source cloud computing platform. Heat enables users to orchestrate and manage OpenStack resources using templates written in the Heat Orchestration Template (HOT) format or YAML. Heat's key strength is its native integration with OpenStack, providing robust orchestration capabilities within OpenStack environments. It's particularly valuable for private cloud setups based on OpenStack, where it simplifies resource provisioning and management.

TYPES OF INFRASTRUCTURE AS CODE

There are two types of IaC and they are the imperative and declarative approaches.

Imperative infrastructure as code   Imperative IaC can be defined as a methodical or step-by-step approach to specifying infrastructure. With this method, the precise steps that must be followed to provide and configure resources are specified. It's comparable to creating a script that specifies each step necessary to bring about a desired outcome.

For example, in imperative IaC, you might write code that says:

- Create a new Lambda function.
- Define the triggers for the function (e.g. an API gateway or an S3 bucket).
- Configure environment variables.
- Set up permissions and security policies.
- Deploy the code to the Lambda function.

This approach can be beneficial when dealing with complicated, multi-step jobs or when you need fine-grained control over the provisioning process. However, it can also be more error-prone and harder to maintain because it requires you to manage the order of operations and handle potential failures explicitly.

Declarative infrastructure as code   On the other hand, declarative IaC focuses on describing the final state of your infrastructure without specifying the precise steps to get there. You define what you want the infrastructure to look like rather than specifying the activities to be executed and the IaC tool works out how to make it happen.

For example, in declarative IaC, you might express your infrastructure requirements like this:

> I want a Lambda function triggered by an API gateway, with specific environment variables and permissions.

Declarative IaC is frequently regarded as being more logical and error-free because it specifies the 'what' rather than the 'how'. Your declarations are interpreted by the IaC tool, which also manages the provisioning and configuration processes. When working with large-scale or regularly changing environments, this strategy is quite helpful for streamlining infrastructure management.

CHOOSING BETWEEN IMPERATIVE AND DECLARATIVE IAC

The decision between imperative and declarative IaC depends on a number of factors, including the complexity of your infrastructure, the preferences of your team and the nature of your use case. In many instances a hybrid approach is used in which declarative IaC is used to specify the general infrastructure architecture, and imperative scripts are used for fine-grained operations.

The following code snippet shows how to define an AWS Lambda function triggered by an API Gateway, with specific environment variables and permissions in Terraform.

```
provider "aws" {
region = var.aws_region
}

# Create an API Gateway REST API
resource "aws_api_gateway_rest_api" "my_api" {
name = "my-api"
description = "My API Gateway"
}

# Define an API Gateway resource
resource "aws_api_gateway_resource" "my_resource" {
parent_id = aws_api_gateway_rest_api.my_api.root_resource_
id
path_part = "myresource"
rest_api = aws_api_gateway_rest_api.my_api.id
}

# Create an AWS Lambda function
resource "aws_lambda_function" "my_lambda" {
function_name = "my-lambda"
runtime = "nodejs12.x"
handler = "index.handler"
source_code_hash = filebase64("./path-to-your-lambda-code")

environment = {
 MY_ENV_VARIABLE = "my-value"
}
}

# Configure permissions for the Lambda function to be
triggered by API Gateway
resource "aws_lambda_permission" "api_gateway_lambda_
permission" {
action = "lambda:InvokeFunction"
function_name = aws_lambda_function.my_lambda.function_
name
```

```
principal = "apigateway.amazonaws.com"
source_arn = "${aws_api_gateway_rest_api.my_api.execution_
arn}/*/*"
}

# Create an API Gateway method to invoke the Lambda
function
resource "aws_api_gateway_method" "my_method" {
authorization = "NONE"
http_method = "POST"
resource_id = aws_api_gateway_resource.my_resource.id
rest_api_id = aws_api_gateway_rest_api.my_api.id
}

# Create an API Gateway integration for the Lambda function
resource  "aws_api_gateway_integration" "my_integration" {
http_method  = aws_api_gateway_method.my_method.
http_method
resource_id  = aws_api_gateway_resource.my_resource.id
rest_api_id  = aws_api_gateway_rest_api.my_api.id
type  = "AWS_PROXY"
uri  = aws_lambda_function.my_lambda.invoke_arn
}

# Create an API Gateway deployment
resource "aws_api_gateway_deployment" "my_deployment" {
rest_api_id = aws_api_gateway_rest_api.my_api.id
description = "My API Gateway Deployment"
}

# Create a stage (e.g., "prod") for the deployment
resource "aws_api_gateway_stage" "my_stage" {
deployment_id = aws_api_gateway_deployment.my_
deployment.id
rest_api_id = aws_api_gateway_rest_api.my_api.id
stage_name = "prod"
}
```

```
# Output the API Gateway URL for the Lambda function
output "api_url" {
value =
"${aws_api_gateway_deployment.my_deployment.invoke_
url}${aws_api_gateway_stage.my_stage.stage_name}"
}
```

Monitoring, logging and performance optimization

Monitoring, logging and performance optimization are also important concepts for promoting the health of your application in the cloud.

MONITORING

Monitoring your cloud infrastructure, applications and services involves continuously tracking a variety of metrics and characteristics. This covers many things, such as CPU and memory utilization, network traffic and response times. This data is gathered and analysed in real time by monitoring tools, which provide warnings when defined thresholds are surpassed or anomalies are found. Because it gives you insight into the state and functionality of your cloud resources, monitoring is important. It enables you to foresee problems like server outages, increasing traffic or unusual activity. Early identification makes it easier to prevent service interruptions and guarantees high availability.

WHAT IS AVAILABILITY IN THE CLOUD?

Availability in the cloud refers to the measure of how consistently and reliably a cloud service or resource is accessible and operational. To understand this concept, let's draw a parallel with Wi-Fi.

When we subscribe to an internet service, we expect to be able to access the internet whenever we need it. However, there are times when we might notice that the Wi-Fi signal is not as strong as usual, or we experience brief interruptions. This happens because even internet service providers, who provide our Wi-Fi, cannot guarantee 100 per cent uptime due to various factors.

Similarly, cloud services use a metric known as 'nines' to quantify their availability. For example, when you hear someone mention 'five nines' availability, it means the service is available 99.999 per cent of the time, indicating a very high level of reliability with minimal downtime. On the other hand, 'three nines' availability (99.9 per cent) suggests that there may be some planned or unplanned downtime, though it is still considered quite reliable.

The more 'nines' a cloud service has in its availability percentage, the closer it is to being available continuously without interruptions. Achieving a higher number of nines often requires robust infrastructure, redundancy and advanced fault-tolerance mechanisms to ensure minimal downtime and maintain uninterrupted access to cloud resources and services.

You don't want to find out about negative news concerning your service on social media through the posts of frustrated customers. Monitoring helps you proactively catch things. Nothing is ever 100 per cent and sometimes systems go bad. It's important to have an on-call engineering team that monitors systems and, when there's an issue, works to mitigate that before the impact becomes terrible.

Now imagine you live in a busy city and you're the owner of a popular restaurant where people come to have breakfast right before they go to their offices. Your business relies heavily on a point-of-sale (POS) system, which operates on a cloud-based platform. Every day, customers come in for their favourite breakfast and your staff uses the POS system to process transactions seamlessly.

Scenario 1 – without monitoring (unaware of issues): In this scenario, you've neglected to implement robust monitoring for your cloud-based POS system. One busy morning, your restaurant is bustling with customers and the demand for your products is exceptionally high. However, unbeknownst to you, your cloud infrastructure is struggling to handle the increased transaction load.

Customers start to experience delays at the checkout, leading to frustration. Some abandon their orders and others voice their complaints on social media. Meanwhile, your employees are unable to process orders efficiently, resulting in longer wait times and stressed-out staff.

You only become aware of these issues when customers begin posting negative reviews online and your restaurant's reputation takes a hit. By the time you realize the problem, you've already suffered damage to your brand.

Scenario 2 – with monitoring (proactive issue detection): In this scenario, you've implemented robust monitoring tools for your cloud-based POS system. As the morning rush begins, your monitoring system immediately detects an unusually high transaction volume and an increase in response times.

Alerts are sent to your on-call team, who swiftly identify the issue – a surge in demand exceeding your system's capacity. They quickly scale up the necessary cloud resources to accommodate the load, ensuring that transactions continue to process smoothly.

Customers notice the seamless service and minimal wait times, leaving your restaurant satisfied. Your online reputation remains positive and your business continues to thrive during peak hours.

Which scenario would you prefer to be your reality?

LOGGING

Logging is the practice of keeping a record of all system operations, events and actions within your cloud environment. This can involve interactions with users, issues with applications, security incidents and administrative adjustments. Logs are a crucial tool for troubleshooting and auditing because they provide a thorough record of what happened and when. Logs are essential for troubleshooting problems, looking into security occurrences and upholding compliance. They offer a historical backdrop for the happenings, assisting you in comprehending the series of events that resulted in a specific result. Logging is crucial for maintaining the integrity and security of cloud systems.

Think of a popular grocery store in your area (let's say Ebeano, Roban Stores, Walmart or Tesco). Now imagine you own a similar store and you decide to install security cameras to monitor the activities in and around your store. These cameras constantly record everything that happens, both inside and outside the store.

One day, you notice that some of your inventory has gone missing and you're not sure why. You and some of your staff decide to review the footage from your security cameras to investigate. As you go through the recorded video, you discover a suspicious individual entering the store and discreetly taking items without paying. Thanks to the video evidence, you're able to identify the person and, with this information, you can take appropriate action, such as reporting the incident or implementing better security measures.

In this scenario, your security cameras serve as logs in the physical world. They provide a detailed record of events and actions, helping you troubleshoot issues (the missing inventory), investigate security incidents (the theft) and maintain compliance with store policies (ensuring customers pay for items). Without these 'logs' you might never have known what happened or who was responsible.

In the context of the cloud, logs also play a similar role. They record all system operations, events and actions, enabling cloud administrators to troubleshoot technical problems, investigate security breaches and ensure that the application adheres to compliance regulations. Just as the security camera footage helped you maintain the security and integrity of your physical store, logs are essential for preserving the reliability and security of cloud systems. They provide a historical record that allows you to understand the sequence of events leading to specific outcomes, much like reviewing the recorded video from your security cameras.

PERFORMANCE OPTIMIZATION

To operate efficiently in the cloud, it's imperative to fine-tune the performance of your infrastructure, applications and services. This optimization revolves around key factors such as resource utilization, response times and cost management. It involves actions such as adjusting resource allocation, implementing load balancing, enabling autoscaling and optimizing your code for efficiency. The ultimate goals are to provide a seamless user experience, control operational expenses and maximize the utilization of resources. Effective performance optimization is the linchpin for meeting user expectations and achieving organizational objectives.

Without adequate optimization, cloud systems can become both costly and unmanageable. Meeting the demands of users and fulfilling business goals hinge on the judicious allocation of resources and ensuring responsive performance. For instance, picture conducting a load test on your application and discovering unacceptably high response times (latency). Such an experience would undoubtedly frustrate your customers. To address this issue, you'd need to implement performance optimization strategies, which might involve refining code, improving resource allocation, or enhancing the scalability of your infrastructure.

Let's take a look at another example. Imagine you run an online store that sells handmade shoes for students. Your website experiences a surge in traffic between June and August every year because parents are looking to buy new shoes for their children to take to school in September. However, as the traffic spikes, you start noticing a significant slowdown in your website's response time. Customers are frustrated by the sluggish performance and some even abandon their shopping carts.

In this scenario, the importance of performance optimization becomes glaringly evident:

- *Lost sales:* The slow website performance leads to a drop in sales. Customers who intended to make purchases abandon their shopping carts due to the frustratingly long loading times. As a result, you're losing revenue.
- *Customer dissatisfaction:* The slow website frustrates your customers, leading to a poor user experience. Unhappy customers are less likely to return to your site in the future, damaging your brand reputation.
- *Increased costs:* To handle the surge in traffic, you might need to provision additional cloud resources on the fly. Without proper optimization, this can lead to skyrocketing operational costs.

Now, let's consider a different scenario where you've invested in performance optimization for your cloud-based infrastructure:

- *Efficient resource allocation:* With proper load balancing and autoscaling mechanisms in place, your website seamlessly handles the traffic surge. Resources are allocated efficiently, preventing unnecessary cost overruns.
- *Happy customers:* Your website's rapid response times delight customers, leading to more completed purchases. Satisfied customers are likely to return and word-of-mouth recommendations further boost your sales.
- *Cost control:* Because your cloud infrastructure is optimized to handle peak loads efficiently, you save on operational costs. You're not paying for excessive resources that sit idle during non-peak periods.

This real-life scenario illustrates that, in the cloud, performance optimization isn't just a technical concern; it directly impacts a business's revenue as well and should be taken very seriously.

REVIEW

This chapter taught you about infrastructure as code, monitoring, logging, performance optimization and cloud engineering. The foundation for modern cloud-based software development and operations is built on these ideas. These aren't simply abstract ideas; they hold the key to maximizing your software development process's effectiveness, dependability and innovation. As we continue in this book (and beyond), remember that cloud engineering and DevOps are not one-size-fits-all solutions; they are adaptable frameworks that you can tailor to your specific needs. As you apply these concepts in your projects, keep in mind the broader picture. Cloud engineering and DevOps are not just about technology; they are about fostering a culture of collaboration, communication and continuous improvement within your teams.

GLOSSARY

ARTIFACT: A compiled or packaged piece of code ready for deployment.

AVAILABILITY: Availability in the cloud refers to the measure of a service's uptime and reliability.

CONFIGURATION MANAGEMENT: The practice of systematically handling changes to a system's configuration, ensuring consistency and reliability.

DEPLOYMENT ENVIRONMENT: The specific target environment where code changes are deployed for testing or production.

INFRASTRUCTURE AS CODE (IAC): IaC involves using code-based approaches to automate the provisioning and management of infrastructure resources required for software deployment.

LOAD BALANCING: Distributing network traffic evenly across multiple servers or resources to prevent overloads.

PROVISIONING: The process of setting up and configuring infrastructure resources such as servers, networks and databases.

SHORTER FEEDBACK LOOPS: Shorter feedback loops reduce the time between making a change and learning its impact. They enable quicker problem resolution, better software quality and efficient responses to user needs.

136

## CHAPTER EIGHT

Platform engineering and no-code tools

As businesses increasingly rely on complicated software systems to power their operations and services, platform teams and platform engineering have grown significantly in popularity in recent times. No-code platforms are also rapidly gaining recognition for their potential to transform application development within organizations. This chapter will go into the fundamentals of platform engineering, illuminating its principles, methods and importance. In this chapter, we'll also explore the profound impact of automation through no-code tools on the cloud engineering and DevOps landscape. These tools go beyond app creation, automating intricate workflows and complex business processes. We'll discuss their benefits and limitations, ensuring a balanced perspective. By the end of this chapter, you'll have a solid understanding of how no-code tools can enhance efficiency in DevOps and cloud engineering. This knowledge will empower you to make informed strategic decisions about developer platforms and no-code tools.

Platform engineering overview

Platform engineering is the discipline of designing and creating toolchains and workflows that provide self-service capabilities for software engineering teams. Platform engineering seeks to improve developer productivity by decreasing the complexity and uncertainty associated with modern software delivery. It addresses some of the most difficult aspects of scaling DevOps, such as aligning development methods with business priorities and lowering the burden of managing a complex web of tools and infrastructure across the entire life cycle of an application.

The platform engineering team's most important role is to build and maintain an integrated product called the internal developer platform (IDP), which is a central collection of tools, services and automated workflows that support the rapid development and delivery of software products across the organization. IDPs act as a service layer, abstracting the complicated aspects of application configuration and infrastructure administration.

Why have internal developer platforms become important?

IDPs have become crucial due to the increasing complexity of software setups. Initially, DevOps aimed to address error-prone and chaotic deployments, leading to improvements in scalability, availability and operability. However, as systems evolved, setups grew more intricate, requiring mastery of multiple tools and technologies.

Many companies embraced the 'You build it, you run it' concept in this context, with developers expected to control the full application life cycle, from development through operations. While this technique works for larger tech firms, it is difficult for other organizations because they may not have access to the same talent pool or the same level of resources to invest in just enhancing their developer workflows and experience.

True DevOps implementation frequently leads to anti-patterns in which developers take on operational responsibilities, resulting in the concept of 'shadow operations'. This situation can reduce productivity because the engineers in charge have to divert their attention away from key development work in order to manage infrastructure and environments.

The presence of an IDP team is the primary distinction between high-performing and low-performing organizations. Many firms are now establishing platform teams dedicated to building IDPs, which let developers choose the level of abstraction they are comfortable with.

HOW DO SOFTWARE DEVELOPERS USE INTERNAL DEVELOPER PLATFORMS?

IDPs seamlessly integrate into the established workflows of application developers, typically centred around a familiar 'Git-push deploy' paradigm. However, IDPs take this workflow to the next level by introducing advanced automation capabilities. Developers retain the convenience of the Git-push deploy model, but they gain greater autonomy and control over the entire deployment pipeline.

Developers can easily request resources such as compute instances, databases or networking configurations within the IDP environment, eliminating the need for manual intervention or resource allocation processes. These resources are delivered quickly and consistently, enabling developers to create fully customized environments tailored to their individual requirements. Developers can also use the IDP platform to start deployments, designate target environments and establish deployment automation rules. This automation reduces the possibility of human error and speeds up the delivery of new features and upgrades.

In case of issues or the need to revert to a previous state, developers have the capability to perform rollbacks directly through the IDP, ensuring system stability and rapid issue resolution. This level of self-service empowerment empowers developers to streamline their workflows, reduce dependencies on other teams and maintain a fast-paced, agile development cycle.

FIGURE 8.1   Workflow with IDP

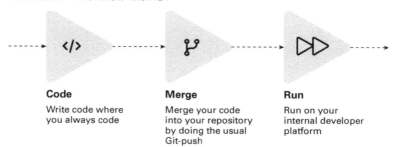

Code

Write code where
you always code

Merge

Merge your code
into your repository
by doing the usual
Git-push

Run

Run on your
internal developer
platform

Benefits of platform engineering

Some benefits of internal developer platforms are:

- *Accelerated development:* IDPs help to accelerate the software development process. IDPs significantly reduce the hassle of manually setting up and configuring infrastructure by providing developers with pre-configured environments and resources. This shortened onboarding process saves developers a substantial amount of time that they would otherwise spend going through the difficulties of infrastructure configuration. As a result, development cycles have accelerated significantly. Developers can quickly begin writing and testing their applications by making use of the widely available, standardized settings. This improves not only individual developer productivity but also team agility, allowing firms to respond quickly to changing business requirements.
- *Competitive advantage:* IDPs can be game changers for firms looking to excel in technology today. These businesses can not only accelerate software delivery but also improve its reliability by employing IDPs. This dual advantage becomes a powerful weapon for attaining a market competitive advantage.
- *Consistency:* IDPs play an important role in ensuring consistency and cohesion among development teams. IDPs enable

developers to work with a common set of tools and configurations by providing standardized development environments. This not only reduces the dreaded compatibility issues that sometimes affect collaborative projects, but also significantly improves the general quality of the codebase. With consistency in place, teams can cooperate and share code without having to adjust to different contexts. This simplifies the development process, encourages cross-team collaboration and shortens project durations. Furthermore, because compatibility-related issues are reduced, developers may devote more time and energy to innovation and feature development, eventually benefiting the business and its end customers.

The work of platform engineering teams

Recently, I've been seeing open roles for this job title: Software engineer – developer platforms. In a role like this, you'd mostly likely be joining a platform engineering team so it's important to know what the team actually does. Beyond building internal developer platforms, platform engineering teams play a multi-faceted role in ensuring the efficiency and success of software development within organizations. One critical issue is standardizing and securing critical delivery processes. This involves creating standardized workflows and procedures to streamline the development, testing and deployment of code. Platform engineers establish a unified and uniform development environment, which reduces error risk, accelerates time to market and improves overall code quality.

Setting and maintaining internal service level agreements (SLAs) is another critical responsibility. Platform engineering teams create precise SLAs that explain the internal developer platform's intended performance, availability and dependability. These SLAs serve as critical benchmarks for assessing the platform's effectiveness and ensuring it satisfies the needs of the enterprise. Furthermore, they serve as a foundation for communication between platform engineers and development teams, promoting transparency and responsibility.

Another key responsibility of platform engineering teams is to monitor team performance metrics. These teams can obtain insights into how development teams use the internal developer platform by collecting and evaluating performance statistics. This includes keeping track of essential metrics like development velocity, deployment frequency and issue resolution time. Platform engineers can use performance data to identify bottlenecks, areas for improvement and chances for optimization, resulting in more efficient and productive development processes.

Platform engineering teams are also critical in cultivating a culture of continuous improvement. They evaluate the performance of the internal developer platform on a regular basis, looking for ways to improve its features, capabilities and user experience. This iterative approach ensures that the platform is always in sync with changing company goals and industry best practices.

On top of that, platform engineers work directly with development teams to understand their individual needs and pain areas. Platform engineering teams can modify the internal developer platform to better match the organization's unique workflows and objectives by actively requesting feedback and addressing the needs of development teams.

These teams also invest in keeping up to date with emerging technologies and trends, ensuring that the internal developer platform remains innovative and capable of adapting to changing software development processes. This dedication to continuous learning and research enables platform developers to bring new tools, procedures and best practices that increase efficiency and effectiveness.

THE 'GLUE'

Platform engineering teams act as the glue between different teams and departments within the organization. They serve as a bridge between development, operations and other functional areas, promoting communication and alignment of objectives. Collaboration ensures that the internal developer platform meets the diverse needs of the organization and enables cross-functional teams to work harmoniously toward common goals.

Do you need a platform engineering team?

Before getting to the point where you build a platform engineering team, the first step is to evaluate whether you actually need one. The need for a platform engineering team is determined by many important elements that correspond with your organization's context and goals. First, you should look at the scope and complexity of your tasks. If your organization is managing multiple teams working on large distributed projects that require complex engineering solutions, or if you're working with cross-functional teams overseeing aspects like application development, operations and infrastructure, it's time to consider building a platform team. This is especially important if you've been relying on ad hoc platform engineering initiatives.

A mature product and a clear vision for its future course can also be strong evidence that a platform team is important. Having a platform team in place can greatly help you achieve your goals of scaling up operations and expanding your products.

In addition, closely observe the nature of your engineering activities. If your engineering teams are heavily involved in cloud integrations and infrastructure operations, it frequently highlights the potential benefits of forming a platform team to successfully streamline these responsibilities.

It is more dependent on the maturity of your product and your preparedness to scale. If your company is relatively small, with only a few engineers working on a monolithic program, the immediate benefits of a platform team may be limited. In such circumstances, prioritize product–market fit and focus on automating repetitive operations to free up your developers to focus on innovation. A platform team can become a powerful catalyst for achieving the delicate balance between speed and stability in your operations when your organization has broken down your application into distinct services, with multiple engineering teams catering to diverse value streams.

No-code tools in cloud engineering

A significant change has occurred in software development and cloud engineering in recent years, all thanks to a powerful and accessible technology: no-code tools.

No-code tools are platforms and software programs that make it possible for users, including those without considerable technical experience, to create and deploy applications in a straightforward and visual manner. They replace traditional programming with drag-and-drop interfaces, pre-built components and logic setups. This democratization of software development and release is opening up new opportunities and speeding up the release of digital solutions.

No-code tools make application development and deployment accessible to a broader audience beyond engineering teams. With these tools, business analysts, designers and domain experts can actively participate in the creation and automation of software solutions. They empower individuals to translate ideas directly into functional applications, reducing the traditional reliance on technical teams and expediting the development cycle.

The intersection of no-code in cloud engineering and DevOps

In recent years, the emergence of no-code tools in cloud engineering has sparked significant interest and innovation. These tools have opened up exciting possibilities for cloud-native development by allowing users, regardless of their coding expertise, to swiftly build and deploy applications on major cloud providers such as AWS, Azure, GCP, DigitalOcean, Kubernetes and more.

What makes this intersection particularly interesting is how well it coincides with the key DevOps principles. At its core, DevOps aims to improve collaboration, automate procedures and speed the delivery of high-quality software. With their capacity to democratize application development and automation, no-code platforms fit seamlessly into this narrative.

Imagine a situation where a cross-functional DevOps team made up of programmers, operations experts and business analysts must produce a new cloud-based application. Individuals from a variety of backgrounds can actively engage in the design, development and deployment of the application using no-code technologies. Within the same platform, developers can focus on developing sophisticated components while operations specialists configure cloud infrastructure. This simultaneous collaboration breaks down silos, promotes openness and speeds up the development process.

In addition, no-code tools' quick prototyping capabilities are well aligned with DevOps' emphasis on continuous integration and delivery. Teams can swiftly prototype and iterate on applications, get stakeholder feedback and make changes in real time. This agility guarantees that the given solution effectively satisfies changing business requirements.

In the context of cloud engineering, no-code solutions enable the development of cloud-native applications and infrastructure setups without the need for considerable manual coding. This not only speeds up the development period but also lowers the danger of human error in complex cloud configurations. Furthermore, these tools frequently include monitoring and analytics functions, which enable the DevOps methodology of continuous monitoring and feedback loops for optimization.

Benefits of no-code tools in cloud engineering

There are a lot of advantages in using no-code tools in cloud engineering. Some of them are listed below:

- *More cloud opportunities:* The integration of no-code tools into cloud engineering has expanded opportunities for entry-level cloud roles. These positions are now accessible to individuals without extensive coding experience but with a strong interest in cloud technologies. They can contribute to organizations by using these tools to manage and deploy cloud infrastructure. This makes learning about cloud infrastructure easier for them and they can continue to grow in their career and take on more challenging parts of cloud engineering.

- *Accelerated development:* No-code platforms are transforming cloud engineering by allowing for rapid application development without the need for serious coding. This acceleration is ideal for the fast-paced software companies, allowing engineers to concentrate on innovation rather than coding complexities. This change allows people from many backgrounds to contribute effectively to cloud projects, fostering team diversity. The reduced coding burden encourages innovation and efficiency in cloud engineering. This disruptive integration of no-code solutions shortens development cycles and provides adaptability in an ever-changing technological context. It's a game changer in cloud engineering.

- *Innovation:* Cloud engineering is being streamlined by no-code solutions, allowing development teams to move their focus away from typical programming responsibilities and toward innovation and user experience enhancement. This abstraction of technological difficulties improves development cycles by allowing teams to allocate more time and resources where they are most needed.

Drawbacks of no-code tools in cloud engineering

While there are benefits in using no-code tools in the context of cloud engineering, it's important to also acknowledge the drawbacks:

- *Complex integrations with older systems:* When organizations attempt to combine no-code applications with legacy systems or other third-party applications, technical difficulties may occur. For example, if a company wishes to integrate a no-code application with an existing business intelligence system, it may have difficulties with data mapping and synchronization. Some no-code apps are designed to export and share data effectively, but when it comes to integrating event triggers, business logic or workflows, many software solutions fall short.
- *Limited customization:* No-code platforms are designed for simplicity and speedy development. However, this frequently implies they have customization constraints. Within the restrictions of these systems, complex or highly specialized solutions may be difficult to build.
- *Lack of scalability:* Large-scale and sophisticated projects may be difficult for no-code tools to handle. As program complexity and user traffic increase, performance and scalability concerns may arise, prompting a return to more traditional development methodologies.

REVIEW

Platform engineering is an evolving concept, but there are a few things available to get you and your team started with this new framework. The platform engineering community on platformengineering.org is available for you to learn more and share the things you learn. In this chapter, we introduced platform engineering and explored how it can improve DevOps. Armed with this knowledge, you can begin to explore, implement and collaborate to harness the full benefits of this evolving framework within your organization.

No-code tools have a chance to grow its impact by also integrating with emerging technologies. We've looked at no-code tools in the context of cloud engineering throughout this chapter, highlighting how these solutions ease the complexities of cloud-related operations. No-code technologies enable individuals and teams to accomplish complicated cloud activities with ease by eliminating the need for extensive coding skills. This trend to no-code not only lowers entry barriers but also promotes cloud adoption and innovation.

GLOSSARY

DEPLOYMENT FREQUENCY: The rate at which software changes, updates or new features are deployed into a production environment. High deployment frequency is a characteristic of agile and DevOps practices, enabling rapid software delivery.

DEVELOPMENT VELOCITY: The speed at which a development team delivers new features, updates or improvements. Development velocity is often used as a key performance indicator to measure a team's productivity.

INTERNAL DEVELOPER PLATFORM (IDP): An integrated product built and maintained by the platform engineering team. It provides a central collection of tools, services and automated workflows that facilitate rapid software development and delivery.

PLATFORM ENGINEERING: The discipline of designing and creating toolchains and workflows that offer self-service capabilities for software engineering organizations. It aims to improve developer productivity by simplifying modern software delivery.

SELF-SERVICE: A capability that allows developers to independently request and manage resources, environments and configurations without manual intervention. Self-service features are a hallmark of internal developer platforms.

TOOLCHAIN: A set of software tools and services that work together to support various stages of software development and delivery. In platform engineering, toolchains are designed to enhance developer productivity and automate workflows.

WORKFLOW: A defined sequence of steps and tasks that outline how work is accomplished. In platform engineering, workflows often include automated processes for deploying, testing and delivering software.

## CHAPTER NINE

Cloud security and privacy

Now more than ever, cloud security has become a very important subject. As the internet grows more and more ingrained in our daily lives and organizations increasingly rely on the cloud for operations, the need to strengthen our digital defences against new threats has become critical. It's not safe to trust that everyone on the internet has good intentions, and the repercussions of poor cloud security can be severe. People have suffered financial losses, fallen victim to account breaches and companies have had their hard-earned credibility damaged as a result of security flaws.

In this chapter, we will cover the best practices, techniques and tools for protecting your data and maintaining the integrity of your digital presence. In a world where digital trust is constantly under risk, this chapter provides you with the information and tools you need to confidently navigate the complicated landscape of cloud security.

Security challenges on the cloud

Let me introduce Obiageli, a young and enthusiastic software developer. She started her career with a desire to create unique cloud apps. Straight out of university, she secured a position at a tech company recognized for its disruptive cloud-based services. She jumped at the chance, joining a vibrant team that was always on the bleeding edge of technology.

Obiageli's first assignment in her new position was to create a new feature for their flagship open-source project. She was ecstatic to be able to contribute to the company after all of her onboarding sessions, and she couldn't wait to dive right into the code. Her project involved integrating a third-party cloud-based service to improve the user experience. It appeared to be a simple task at first, but little did she know that it would lead to one of her most valuable cloud security learning experiences.

She first hardcoded the API key to get the feature working for a team demo because she was eager to move swiftly. It appeared to be a time-saving shortcut that would allow her to impress her team on demo day when it was her turn to present what she had worked on all week.

However, as Obiageli dug more into the project, she realized the significance of optimal security measures. Recognizing the dangers of leaving sensitive information exposed in the code-base, she resolved to correct her error but was too afraid to tell anyone what she had previously done. She modified the program to use the API key from a secure secrets manager before submitting her pull request for the feature.

While this modification fixed the immediate security issue, Obiageli made an innocent miscalculation. She didn't realize the initial commit, which included the hardcoded API key, was still in the commit history. Despite the fact that she had removed the exposed key from the current code, the sensitive information was still available through the commit logs.

A few weeks later, her team received an alarming notification: illegal access to their cloud services had occurred. Panicked, they started an investigation to figure out the source of the breach. It didn't take long during the investigation to link the dots back to Obiageli's earlier mistake. Despite the fact that the API key was no longer being used directly through code, it was identified in the commit history and used by a malicious actor, resulting in unauthorized access to their cloud infrastructure.

Obiageli was upset by her mistake, but she was determined to make amends and learn from it. She went to the company learning portal and discovered some basic security courses to help her learn before her next project. Her experience shone a light on some of the most prevalent security issues seen in cloud environments.

SECURITY CHALLENGE 1: INSECURE COMMIT HISTORY

Obiageli's unintended inclusion of API keys in the commit history exemplifies a common problem in software development. When sensitive information, such as passwords, keys or access tokens, are exposed in a commit, the implications can be severe. Malicious actors and automated bots are continually searching repositories for such data. As a result, Obiageli's experience emphasizes the importance of sophisticated security scanning tools that can automatically discover and redact sensitive information before it is committed. Developers should also be taught the necessity of never hardcoding sensitive information directly into code.

SECURITY CHALLENGE 2: IRREGULAR KEY ROTATION

The incident involving Obiageli serves as a reminder of the significance of regular key rotation. To restrict the exposure window of critical credentials, cloud providers often advocate frequent key rotation. Failure to follow this approach can result in serious vulnerabilities in security. To reduce human mistakes, teams should implement tight key rotation procedures and automate the process if possible. In addition, it is critical that the procedure for changing keys be well-documented and easily available to all team members.

SECURITY CHALLENGE 3: LACK OF VIGILANCE IN CODE REVIEW

Obiageli's experience emphasizes the importance of code review in ensuring security. Code reviews should encompass more than just functional features; they should also include security checks. To uncover potential vulnerabilities and security flaws in the codebase, developers should use specialized security scanning tools. On top of that, developing a security-conscious culture among engineers is critical. Regular training and awareness programmes can assist in ensuring that all team members understand the significance of security in every code change.

SECURITY CHALLENGE 4: INCIDENT RESPONSE

Obiageli's situation highlights the need of having a robust incident response plan in place. When there is a security breach, a quick and organized response is critical. The roles and responsibilities should be clearly defined in incident response plans, including who to call, what steps to take and how to communicate both internally and publicly. Obiageli's experience also emphasizes the significance of rolling and replacing compromised keys as part of the incident response procedure.

HAVE YOU EVER BEEN AN OBIAGELI AT YOUR JOB?

Obiageli's story is a good lesson for young developers just starting out in the field of cloud engineering. It serves as a warning that in the complicated cloud world, even seemingly slight oversights can lead to substantial security concerns. Developers like Obiageli may transform their failures into opportunities for growth and improvement in cloud security if they are determined and committed to constant learning.

Beyond these security challenges discovered by Obiageli, there are other security challenges in the cloud that we should be aware of as professionals that interact with the cloud daily. These encompass a wide range of issues, each requiring a tailored approach to mitigation.

Data breaches and data loss

One of the most serious concerns in cloud security is the looming threat of data breaches and data loss. These risks loom enormous and have the potential to wreak havoc on businesses, resulting in disastrous implications that transcend far beyond the field of cyber security.

Even the most cautious businesses can fall victim to data breaches because they act like sneaky intruders and can get past their security measures. They are frequently caused by a combination of different things. Weak access controls are a typical entry point for attackers. Inadequately managing permissions allows attackers to take advantage of the service to obtain unauthorized access to sensitive data. Beyond access control, the absence of robust encryption mechanisms can also cause data breaches. When sensitive data like passwords, card PINs or tokens are not properly encrypted during data transmission or while at rest, they become easy prey for cybercriminals. Passwords that are weak or simple to guess can also potentially invite attackers in. Cybercriminals use password flaws to obtain unauthorized access to cloud accounts and the vast amounts of data they store.

The issues above can cause data breaches, but unfortunately, sometimes the problem isn't an external attacker. The root cause can be traced back to a seemingly innocuous yet critical factor: human error or oversight. Misconfigured settings, either in haste or due to a lack of understanding, can expose sensitive data to the public or unauthorized individuals. Misconfigured settings in a company's digital infrastructure are one of the most typical examples of this oversight. These settings can mistakenly be set in a way that exposes sensitive data to the public or unauthorized individuals, whether as a result of a hurried deployment process or a lack of thorough understanding of the technology in use. Consider a situation where a system administrator who is well-intentioned but in a hurry quickly configures access permissions for a cloud storage server. They can unintentionally offer more access privileges than they meant to in their haste to get things up and running, making sensitive files and data accessible to a larger audience than they had originally intended. Similar to this, unintentional vulnerabilities might result from a lack of thorough understanding of the nuances of security procedures and data management. For instance, an employee may unintentionally configure a database with insufficient encryption, thinking it is sufficiently secure, only to learn later that confidential client information is susceptible to theft. These errors, whether the result of a hasty decision or a lack of knowledge, can have serious repercussions. They open the door for data breaches by making it extremely simple for unauthorized parties, including cybercriminals, to access private information without trying too hard.

Data loss, on the other hand, frequently occurs within a company, yet the results can be just as disastrous. Imagine the agony of learning that crucial data was accidentally deleted by a well-intentioned employee rather than a malicious cyber attacker. These unintentional deletions may cause important data or resources to be permanently lost. Even cloud services can experience system failures, such as hardware malfunctions, software problems or outages, which can render data abruptly inaccessible. In such moments, organizations might find themselves struggling with the agonizing reality of irrecoverable data.

Identity and access management risks

Misconfigured identity and access management can result in unauthorized access, which means that someone or something can obtain access to systems, data or resources they should not have. This can be caused by overly permissive regulations or a lack of appropriate restrictions. Privilege escalation is also one of the most serious consequences of identity and access management misconfiguration. This happens when an identity that is supposed to have limited access is able to elevate their privileges. This is comparable to a regular user getting administrator access in the context of cloud security, which is definitely not a good thing.

As a result of unauthorized access and privilege escalation, identity and access management misconfigurations can lead to data exposure. If an identity has overly permissive policies then they have access to data and resources they shouldn't have access to, which means these things are already exposed. Beyond this primary exposure, there is also the possibility that sensitive data may be subject to additional risks and consequences.

Let's look at effects when a user with the access (e.g. a scorned employee in a small organization) intentionally wants to hurt the organization:

- *Data manipulation:* A malicious insider has access to and control over sensitive data. They might change customer data, or product data, which would result in incorrect decisions, financial losses and legal issues.
- *Intellectual property theft:* Such a person could steal proprietary software, trade secrets, designs or other important intellectual property. This could put the organization at a competitive disadvantage.
- *Insider threat investigations:* As a result of suffering data manipulation and theft, the corporation will have to devote significant time and resources to investigating and mitigating the malicious user's behaviour, which will take employees' focus away from core business activities.

This might not be the case for larger organizations, but malicious attackers get more creative every day and as part of an organization (or someone looking to build an organization someday), you should be aware of these issues and how they affect you, so that you can handle things proactively.

We've seen what happens when a user with access has malicious intentions. But there's another possibility. Imagine what happens when a user with access has good intentions but is vulnerable and gets hacked:

- *Data breach:* Even if a user has good intentions, cybercriminals can get access to sensitive data if the user's credentials are compromised due to a vulnerability. This can lead to data breaches and the disclosure of sensitive information.
- *Loss of trust:* Customers, partners and stakeholders may lose trust in the organization if their data is compromised as a result of a hack, resulting in reputational harm and legal penalties.
- *Costly remediation:* The organization will incur costs as a result of the breach, such as investigating the breach, deploying security patches and maybe compensating affected parties.
- *Regulatory penalties:* The organization may incur regulatory fines and penalties for failing to appropriately protect sensitive data, depending on the severity of the breach and applicable data protection regulations.

Regardless of whether users have good or bad intentions, employees shouldn't have unlimited and unauthorized access to resources. It's too risky to give that much power to anyone.

Distributed denial of service attacks

Another security challenge in the cloud is distributed denial of service (DDoS) attacks. As the cloud makes services accessible over the internet, it has also become easy for malicious cyber attackers to disrupt online services by inundating them with a flood of traffic, rendering them slow or entirely unavailable to legitimate users. The consequence of this is a significant disruption in service availability, leading to customer dissatisfaction.

DDoS attacks usually entail an organized effort to saturate the target system, network or application with traffic. To create large volumes of traffic, attackers frequently use botnets, which are networks of compromised computers that are under their control. This influx of traffic can easily exhaust the target's bandwidth and computational capacity, rendering the service slow or totally unusable.

A successful DDoS assault may have devastating effects. Businesses may suffer significant financial losses as a result of downtime, particularly if the attacked service is essential for generating revenue. The reputational harm may also persist for a long time, reducing customer confidence and trust. If customer data or other sensitive information is compromised during an attack, regulatory organizations may in some situations impose fines or penalties.

Compliance and legal issues

Given that different sectors and geographic locations put unique requirements on businesses, maintaining compliance with the different data handling and storage standards is a challenge. Failure to adhere to these compliance requirements can have serious repercussions, such as legal penalties, harm to one's reputation and large fines. To successfully navigate this, everyone must constantly be informed of the essential compliance frameworks that are applicable to their sector and geographical area. Here are just some examples:

- The General Data Protection Regulation (GDPR), which is intended to protect the personal data of inhabitants of the European Union, is one of the most well-known examples of data protection laws. The GDPR's data protection rules must be strictly followed by organizations that process or keep the personal data of EU individuals, or they run the risk of incurring heavy financial penalties. For instance, failure to comply may result in fines of up to €20 million, or 4 per cent of the organization's annual global revenue, whichever is more.

- Service Organization Control 2 (SOC 2), which assesses the security, availability, processing integrity, confidentiality and privacy of customer data, is frequently required of service organizations. Businesses can assure their clients that their data is handled with the highest care by achieving SOC 2 compliance.
- The Nigeria Data Protection Regulation (NDPR), which was introduced in 2019, is Nigeria's equivalent of a data protection law. It specifies the rules and criteria for data protection that businesses must adhere to when handling personal data in Nigeria.
- There are also data protection regulations in the United States, although the laws differ greatly from state to state. As an example, California uses the California Consumer Privacy Act (CCPA) for data privacy legislation. Due to the potential impact on their business operations, companies with consumers or clients in states like California need to pay special attention to the CCPA.

Best practices for cloud security

The previous section highlighted some of the security challenges in the cloud. Over time, people have created frameworks and best practices that help organizations stay secure as their services exist on the cloud. These best practices help them safeguard their assets, maintain data integrity and ensure that they are always compliant with industry regulations and standards.

Access control

Access control is very important in cloud security because it acts as an important defence against unwanted access to sensitive information and resources. Strong access control techniques are required in the cloud, to keep data safe from breaches and loss.

A key concept in access control is the principle of least privilege. It requires that identities should be given only the minimum level of access or permissions necessary to carry out their particular duties or functions. By following this rule, companies lower their risk of unintentional or malicious exposure of data. As the compromised person or system only has access to a limited subset of resources, it reduces the attack surface and hence limits the potential damage that can happen if an account is compromised.

Another important factor in access control, particularly in cloud contexts, is just-in-time (JIT) access. It involves only allowing access to resources when they are actually required for a given task or period of time. By reducing the time of access and window of risk, JIT improves security. Users are granted brief access for a certain activity or duration, after which it is automatically terminated to minimize the risk of prolonged access.

Access control is made more secure by using multi-factor authentication. Before being granted access to cloud resources, users must present proof of identification at least twice. This usually involves the user's knowledge (like a password), possessions (like a mobile app or hardware token) and identity (like biometric data). Multi-factor authentication greatly improves security by making it exponentially harder for unauthorized parties to access, even if they manage to steal the user's password. As a result, it's crucial to set up multi-factor authentication for each member of your team.

Another very useful and effective technique to manage permissions in cloud systems is role-based access control (RBAC). In RBAC access is given according to employment roles or functions inside an organization. Predefined roles are allocated to users, each of which has a set of permissions. As a result, managing access control is easier because roles can govern permissions rather than individuals. Access may be granted or revoked more

quickly with RBAC, which also ensures that users have the right
amount of privilege for their roles and responsibilities.

ROLE-BASED ACCESS CONTROL IN REAL LIFE

Let's illustrate RBAC in the context of a SaaS company,
considering various types of employees:

- Software developers:
  - Role: 'Developer'
  - Permissions:
    - Read and write access to the source code repositories.
    - Access to development and testing environments.
    - Limited access to production environments for debugging
      and monitoring purposes.
- Senior developers:
  - Role: 'Senior developer'
  - Permissions:
    - All permissions of developers.
    - Authorization to review and approve code merges.
    - Access to more advanced debugging and profiling tools.
- Team leads:
  - Role: 'Team lead'
  - Permissions:
    - All permissions of senior developers.
    - Authority to assign tasks, set priorities and manage the
      development team.
    - Access to deployment tools for pushing code to
      production after review.
- Managers:
  - Role: 'Manager'
  - Permissions:
    - Access to project management and collaboration tools.
    - Oversight of multiple teams and projects.
    - Limited access to financial data for budgeting and
      resource allocation.

- Vice presidents:
  - Role: 'VP'
  - Permissions:
    - Oversight of the entire development department.
    - Access to sensitive HR data for team evaluation and resource planning.
    - Decision-making authority on department-wide initiatives and budgets.
- Quality assurance engineers:
  - Role: 'QA engineer'
  - Permissions:
    - Access to testing environments for running test cases.
    - Ability to file bug reports and request code fixes from developers.
    - Limited access to production environments for testing purposes only.
- Customer support representatives:
  - Role: 'Customer support'
  - Permissions:
    - Access to customer support tools and databases for issue resolution.
    - Limited access to customer data for verifying customer identities and providing assistance.
    - No access to development or code repositories.
- System administrators:
  - Role: 'Sysadmin'
  - Permissions:
    - Access to organization infrastructure and network resources.
    - Authority to manage user accounts, passwords and security configurations.
    - Limited access to development environments for troubleshooting infrastructure issues.

In this RBAC system, access permissions are granularly tailored to each role's specific responsibilities. Employees with titles like 'developer', 'QA engineer', 'VP' and others are limited to permissions that perfectly match their assigned job tasks as a result. This maintains access privileges in a precise balance with work needs, enhancing security and lowering the risk of abuse or data disclosure.

Encryption

Encryption is very important in cloud security because it offers several levels of security for information kept in the cloud.

To explain the concept of encryption, let's step out of the cloud for a bit and explore a real-life example. I've been in situations where I wanted to pass a confidential message to a friend. In these situations I'd decide to communicate my message with languages or terms that only we understand. This way, I can prevent my message from being intercepted by others during delivery to my friend. In a way, I have secured my communication by employing a language translation method as a form of encryption.

In this scenario, my original message, the plaintext, is something everyone understands. To encode the message, I employ the language translation process as a form of encryption. This step transforms my message into a coded language, rendering it incomprehensible to those who lack knowledge of this specific linguistic code. The translated message becomes the ciphertext, a seemingly random sequence of characters that conceals the true meaning from potential eavesdroppers.

When my friend gets the message, she engages in the decryption process because she possesses the language proficiency required to reverse the translation, unveiling the original, confidential message. This decryption step mirrors the retrieval of the plaintext, completing the cycle of secure communication.

FIGURE 9.1   Encryption process

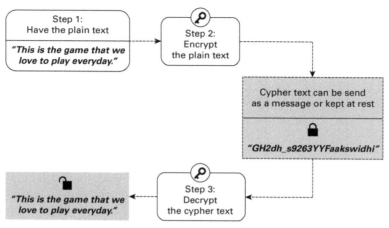

In the cloud, there are more complex algorithms that can be used in encrypting data. Some of them include the widely adopted Advanced Encryption Standard (AES), known for its efficiency and versatility in securing data at rest and in transit. For asymmetric encryption, Rivest-Shamir-Adleman (RSA) and elliptic-curve cryptography (ECC) are important in ensuring secure communications and key exchange processes. Beyond these, there are other algorithms and functions such as Diffie-Hellman Key Exchange, Triple DES (3DES), Blowfish, TwoFish, ChaCha20, hash functions like SHA-256 and hybrid solutions like Pretty Good Privacy (PGP). By using sophisticated algorithms to encrypt the data, which renders it unreadable without the right decryption keys, it protects the data from illegal access. The encrypted data is safe and inaccessible even if an unauthorized person gains access to the physical or virtual infrastructure where it is housed. It is advised that encryption should be done for data in transit as well as data at rest.

Encryption can be either symmetric or asymmetric. In symmetric encryption, the same key is used for encryption and decryption, which makes the process more straightforward.

However, this straightforwardness comes with the challenge of securely managing and distributing the shared key. This is different from asymmetric encryption, where a pair of keys are used instead: a public key for encryption and a private key for decryption. The public key can be freely distributed, allowing anyone to encrypt messages that only the holder of the corresponding private key can decrypt. This method addresses the key distribution challenge in symmetric encryption.

Regular auditing and monitoring

Performing routine audits and monitoring is essential processes for maintaining cloud security. Auditing involves examining the cloud infrastructure, applications and data to ensure that there is compliance with security policies and regulations. Monitoring involves continual tracking of events, actions and system functionality in order to identify and address security incidents as soon as they occur. Monitoring provides real-time visibility into the cloud environment. In a properly monitored system you can detect unusual activities, unauthorized access or other security issues. Promptly identifying these incidents enables rapid response and mitigation, which reduces the impact of the security incident.

To explain the concept of security auditing, I will use financial services as an example. The financial services industry is highly regulated and security audits help the businesses that play in that industry stay compliant. To guarantee the integrity of important financial information, these audits provide a careful examination of an organization's cyber security and cloud infrastructure.

Trust is very important in financial services (if someone asked me to put my money in an organization with a bad reputation, I wouldn't). As customers, we entrust our financial institutions with sensitive information and security auditing provides a way to hold these institutions accountable and ensure adherence to industry regulations such as PCI DSS, Sarbanes-Oxley and others. This alignment with regulatory standards not only mitigates legal risks but also fosters a culture of transparency and trust.

Differences between monitoring and auditing in security:

- Monitoring is real-time and continuous. It provides immediate insights into current security events. Auditing is typically periodic or event-driven and the goal is to gauge compliance and get an in-depth analysis of security practices.

- Monitoring is also more operational and it deals with the day-to-day security landscape and incident response. Auditing is more strategic and involves a comprehensive examination of the organization's security.

Security incident response

In a well-monitored system, you're able to spot security incidents. Having a good security incident response plan is the next step after putting monitoring in place to ensure that you can mitigate issues when they occur. There are several benefits of having a robust security incident response plan.

A company's ability to reduce the effects of security incidents is improved by having a clearly defined incident response plan. The plan typically includes an organized framework for responding to a variety of incidents, from malware assaults to data breaches, by outlining procedures for identification, isolation, mitigation, recovery and learning. By being proactive and planning incident response, security teams can guarantee that problems may be resolved quickly and effectively, minimizing damage and delay.

Another advantage is that an efficient incident response plan encourages organized communication and coordination among everyone on the team involved in the incident. Communication that is accurate and fast is essential in the event of a security incident. A well-organized strategy ensures that everyone in the team is on the same page by defining roles and duties for each team member and opening channels of communication. In addition to promoting a quicker response, this coordination also ensures transparency throughout the incident resolution process.

Continuous learning is part of the job in incident response and it is accomplished through a process known as a post-mortem. The goal of a post-mortem is to assist the team in drawing lessons from previous experiences. It usually entails an analysis shortly after the incident. Knowing the underlying cause of a security issue is crucial for preventing similar ones in the future. As more complex incidents emerge with time, it is important to become knowledgeable about them in order to improve the incident response plan.

STEPS FOR CREATING A SECURITY INCIDENT RESPONSE PLAN

Security incident response is something that should be planned, as opposed to the team being reactive about it. The plan should include what to do at each stage of the incident from when it's identified to when it's resolved. The steps below are a blueprint to guide you in the development of your own plan:

- *Create an incident response team:* Create an incident response team, define roles and responsibilities for each team member and put each team member on a rotation so that they know when and how to go about their duties in the event of an incident. This ensures a coordinated and comprehensive response.
- *Define incident categories and severity levels:* When there is an incident, there is usually a degree of importance and potential impact that varies across different scenarios. To effectively address this variability, identify and categorize potential security incidents based on their nature and potential impact. This involves an examination of the types of incidents

that could occur, considering factors such as data sensitivity, system criticality and the potential consequences of a breach. Once identified, it's important to specify severity levels. Severity levels help prioritize responses, ensuring that the incident response team focuses on the most critical issues first. This prioritization is essential for allocating resources effectively and responding proportionately to incidents based on their potential impact.

- *Define mechanisms for identifying and reporting incidents:* Once the team and the severities have been established, the next thing will be to adopt a monitoring system that can detect potential security incidents in real time. Establishing clear procedures for incident reporting ensures a streamlined response mechanism. This includes defining explicit channels for incidents to be reported. The synergy of a monitoring system and well-defined reporting procedures enhances your team's ability to quickly detect, assess and respond to security incidents.

- *Create documentation for the team:* Whether it's for new or existing team members, documentation about the processes and guides for troubleshooting incidents can help everyone understand the step-by-step procedures for responding to alerts, mitigating, resolving and documenting incidents.

- *Establish an escalation process and coordinate with external entities:* When there is a security incident that surpasses the capabilities of internal response measures, a well-established escalation process guides the organization on when and how to involve higher management or external teams. Furthermore, it is crucial to establish relationships and communication channels with external entities. These relationships form a network of support, ensuring a coordinated and informed response in the face of advanced or widespread incidents.

- *Conduct post-incident analysis:* After resolving an incident, conduct a thorough post-incident analysis to identify lessons learned, opportunities for improvement and potential adjustments to the incident response plan. Based on these findings, revise the plan as needed.

• *Regularly review and update the plan:* Technology is evolving and so are cyber threats. So it's important to regularly review and update your incident response plan based on lessons your team has learned over time, emerging threats and technological changes.

Beyond security incidents, this framework can also be replicated by site reliability engineering (SRE) teams that want to create their own incident response plan for monitoring application availability.

Monitor and protect endpoints

API endpoints should be monitored and protected in order to ensure cloud security. To accomplish this, recommendations include network integrity monitoring and protection for both internal and external endpoints through the adoption of powerful security tools. These security methods act as proactive barriers, detecting and mitigating potential network threats. Adopting industry-standard methodologies is also critical for fortifying defences against popular attacks, such as DDoS attacks. Organizations may build a resilient defence system that protects endpoints from a wide range of potential cyber threats by adding these techniques into their security framework.

DevSecOps

On the cloud, it's important to integrate security with everything including DevOps, as opposed to it being an afterthought. Development, security and operations (DevSecOps) automates the integration of security across the software development life cycle, from initial design to integration, testing, deployment and software delivery.

FIGURE 9.2   DevOps vs DevSecOps

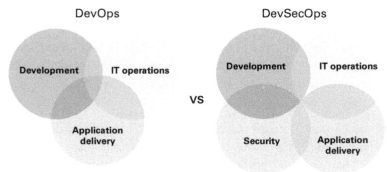

DevSecOps is an evolution in the way software development organizations approach security. Previously, security was checked by a different quality assurance team and added to software at the very end of the development cycle (almost as an afterthought) by a separate security team. When software upgrades were only released once or twice a year, this was acceptable. However, as software engineering teams adopted Agile and DevOps practices, with the goal of shortening software development cycles to weeks or even days, the traditional approach to security became unsustainable.

Application and infrastructure security are easily integrated into Agile and DevOps processes and tools by DevSecOps. As security vulnerabilities arise, it takes care of them when fixing them is simpler, quicker and less expensive. DevSecOps also shifts application and infrastructure security from the primary responsibility of a security silo to the shared responsibility of development, security and IT operations teams.

What are the benefits of DevSecOps?

The three main advantages of integrating DevSecOps are security, speed and collaboration. By integrating security practices into the DevOps workflow, organizations can enhance the over-all security of their applications and the collaboration across teams. These things help teams grow in their ability to deliver secure, high-quality software at a rapid pace, aligning with the demands of today's dynamic and competitive technological landscape.

Developing new features securely   Here are some of the ways that DevSecOps allows teams to develop new features securely:

- *Security is embedded into the CI/CD pipeline.* This ensures that security checks are performed automatically at every stage of development. This continuous integration prevents the introduction of vulnerabilities and allows for immediate remediation.
- *It encourages a shift-left security methodology,* which means that security considerations are handled early in the development life cycle. This proactive approach guarantees that security is not an afterthought in the feature development process, but rather an intrinsic part of it.
- *Automated vulnerability scanning solutions enable teams to identify and address any security concerns in real time.* This accelerates vulnerability discovery and response, reducing the risk of security breaches.
- *Software teams become more conscious of security best practices.* They are more proactive in identifying potential security risks in the application's code, or other technologies.

Faster releases without compromising security   The major way DevSecOps makes releases faster without compromising secu-rity is through automated tests. Here's how:

- With DevSecOps, teams use automation to carry out thorough security tests, making it much less likely for people to make mistakes. They integrate these automated security tests as they build software, so it always looks carefully for any inconsistencies or security vulnerabilities in the code. This not only ensures they find security issues accurately but also speeds up the whole testing process.

- One big benefit of using automated security tests in DevSecOps is that it stops security checks from slowing down the development process. Before, when people checked security manually, it took a lot of time and sometimes caused delays in releasing the software. DevSecOps fixes this by smoothly including automated security testing as a crucial part of the process. This means they can check for security issues at the same time as they're working on other parts of the software, keeping everything moving fast.
- Using automation in security testing helps teams find and fix problems quickly, offering real-time feedback to developers. By catching security issues early on, they can deal with them quickly, which means less time and effort to fix things later.

Fostering a collaborative culture   DevSecOps is also effective at fostering a collaborative and adaptive culture across different teams in various ways:

- It eliminates silos between development, security and operations teams, encouraging a collaborative culture. Cross-functional teams collaborate seamlessly to ensure that security is considered in all stages of development and deployment.
- It encourages a culture of shared security responsibility, with each team member accountable for the overall security posture. This shared ownership encourages a common commitment to developing and maintaining secure applications.
- A culture of constant learning and development is promoted by DevSecOps. Regular retrospectives, post-incident investigations and knowledge-sharing sessions help to foster an adaptable culture by allowing teams to learn from their experiences and improve their security practices over time.

Threat modelling

Better results are achieved in terms of delivery cost and security posture the earlier security is taken into consideration in the development life cycle. You can use threat modelling – the process of securing systems and data through the use of hypothetical scenarios, system diagrams and testing. Threat modelling improves security and trust in cloud systems by finding weaknesses, assisting with risk assessment and recommending corrective measures.

The process of threat modelling involves a few important things:

- *Enhanced view of systems:* Threat modelling helps software engineering teams see their computer systems better. They do this by creating pictures called data flow diagrams (DFDs) and showing how attackers might try to get in. They also figure out which parts of their system are most important and what risks they need to focus on. Doing this helps teams understand their network security and how everything works together.
- *Better collaboration on security:* Doing threat modelling isn't just for one person or team. It needs input from many people who are involved in the computer systems. When everyone takes part, it helps the team all work together better on security. It's like making sure everyone in a team knows how to keep things safe. This way, everyone becomes more aware of cyber security and how important it is for everyone involved.
- *Risk prioritization:* Threat modelling gives teams data about possible threats. With this information, businesses can decide which security risks are more important to deal with first. This helps businesses know where to put their time and money to make sure the most important things are secure. So, threat modelling helps businesses figure out what needs attention the most.

STEPS IN THREAT MODELLING

Executing threat modelling for your computer system involves the following steps:

- *Identify assets:* In threat modelling, the first thing is to figure out what's important to protect. These things are called 'assets'. Assets can be different types of important things, like user data, intellectual property or the entire system functionality.
- *Visualize the system:* The next step is to draw the DFDs. These diagrams show how the computer system works. They help everyone see the important parts and how information moves around. Another type of diagram teams can draw is an attack tree. It shows us where attacks might come from and how they could happen.
- *Identify the threats:* After drawing these diagrams, analyse them closely to see where there might be threats. There are different threat modelling methods to analyse different kinds of threats and this step is important to identify potential threats and risks.
- *Mitigate:* Once everyone is clear on the important things and the risks, teams can come up with what to do to mitigate the risks. For example, they might need to change settings in our firewall, use encryption or add more security steps like multifactor authentication. These steps help everyone fix the identified problems.
- *Validate findings:* After identifying potential threats and deciding on fixes, it's important to check whether the solution works. This step is called validation. It involves testing and verifying that the security measures put in place effectively address the identified threats. Through validation, teams ensure that the chosen fixes enhance the security of their systems.

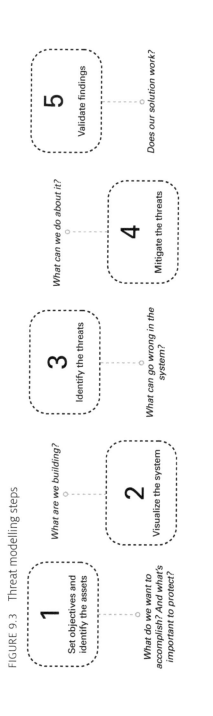

FIGURE 9.3 Threat modelling steps

THREAT MODELLING FRAMEWORKS

- STRIDE (spoofing, tampering, repudiation, information disclosure, denial of service, elevation of privilege)
- DREAD (damage, reproducibility, exploitability, affected users, discoverability)
- PASTA (process for attack simulation and threat analysis)
- OWASP application threat modelling (OWTF)
- TRIKE (threat and risk intelligence knowledgebase)
- VAST (visual, agile and simple threat modelling):
  - Cyber Kill Chain
  - HARA (host and application risk analysis)
  - OCTAVE (operationally critical threat, asset and vulnerability evaluation)

Validating the threat modelling exercise

Measuring how well threat modelling works can be done in two ways.

Common vulnerability scoring system One way is to use the common vulnerability scoring system (CVSS). This system gives standardized scores to vulnerabilities in applications, IT systems and IoT devices. You can easily calculate these scores using a free online tool. To get a better idea, you can compare your scores with a database that collects scores from similar businesses. This helps you see how your security measures stack up against others.

Penetration testing Another way is through something called penetration testing. This involves simulating attacks on a system to understand its strengths and weaknesses. However, these tests can take a bit of time for careful analysis, so it's essential not to do too many or run tests on things that aren't very risky. It's all about finding the right balance between making sure your system is secure and not spending too much time or money on tests that might not be needed.

Identifying code-level vulnerabilities

Identifying code level vulnerabilities is vital for keeping our cloud systems safe. This means carefully analysing the code of the programs we use in the cloud to find any possible weaknesses or gaps in security. Why is this so crucial? Well, when we find and fix these issues early on, it saves a lot of trouble and money compared to dealing with them after we've already set everything up and the stakes are higher.

Additionally, looking for code-level problems is a great way to teach software development teams about potential risks and how to write safe code. This not only makes the code safer but also creates a mindset where everyone is always thinking about how to improve security.

Security architectural patterns

Security architectural patterns are design solutions that address common security challenges in software and system architecture. These patterns provide a structured and proven way to integrate security measures into the design of applications and systems so that we can protect these resources.

A SHORT STORY ABOUT NOT PROPERLY PROTECTING PUBLIC RESOURCES

Let me share a story to explain what can go wrong when we forget to protect public resources. Picture a house with a water supply kept in a bucket in the shared area.

Now, think about a housemate who really needs water. They carefully take some water into their bowl and head back inside. Meanwhile, there's another person around – not a housemate, but someone with access to the water. This person, without thinking about others, uses the water to wash their hands, dirtying the water.

Now, imagine a third person, also a housemate, but not paying much attention. They stroll toward the water, accidentally kicking the bucket. In a flash, all the water is gone.

Why did all this happen? Because we didn't keep a close eye on who could use the water.

How can we make things better? Let's take away the bucket and put it in a safe spot. We'll make the house more secure, so people from outside can't mess with things that are just for housemates. And here's a neat idea – let's add a tap so housemates can get water in a more organized way.

The end.

I've given so many conference talks about security architectural patterns and there is one thing I always say in my presentations. When thinking about security, it's important to ask clarifying questions about the design of the application, as that will inform the secure pattern to inculcate. The answers to these questions build up some sort of checklist. Like the illustration with the housemates shown above, make sure you're accounting for different use cases to prevent problems later, much like the delicate balance of housemates sharing a water supply, ensuring the security of an application involves anticipating various scenarios. As illustrated earlier, where a lack of foresight led to unintended consequences, the same principle applies to the design and security of applications. By posing these clarifying questions upfront, we create a foundation that aligns security measures with the unique characteristics of the application.

Imagine the design process as a series of interconnected rooms in our metaphorical house, each representing a different aspect of the application. By asking questions about who has access, how data flows and what potential risks exist, we navigate the blueprint of the application much like we'd navigate the layout of the house. This approach not only prevents problems down the line but also allows us to tailor security measures to fit seamlessly into the application's structure.

Sample questions to ask when trying to analyse and understand how your application needs to be secured:

- Will my application contain sensitive customer data?
- Where and how is my application's data stored?
- Will this application be available over the internet (publicly) or just internally?
- How do I plan to verify my user's identity?
- What sensitive tasks are performed in my application?
- Does my application perform any risky software activities?

There are many other possible security patterns, but the next section will cover three of them. Each pattern is either for data protection or identity management.

The gatekeeper pattern

Endpoints exposed by cloud services allow client apps to interact with their APIs. The code that implements these APIs is in charge of a variety of tasks. When the application's hosting environment is hacked, the security measures, as well as credentials, storage keys, sensitive data and other services, are exposed. This vulnerability allows malicious actors to get unauthorized access, posing a severe security risk.

To address the security issue, one way is to separate the code responsible for public endpoints from the code responsible for requests and storage access. This decoupling can be accomplished through a dedicated interface that acts as an intermediary between clients and the components that handle requests. The gatekeeper pattern is used to safeguard databases, storage and the entire application.

There are three key features about the gatekeeper pattern:

- All requests are extensively validated by the gatekeeper and those that fail to meet validation requirements are rejected.
- The gatekeeper does not have access to the credentials that the trusted host uses for storage and services. In the event of a breach, the attacker is unable to acquire access to these crucial credentials.
- In order to prevent direct access to application services or data even in the event of a compromise, the gatekeeper operates in a restricted privilege mode. The rest of the application functions in the full trust mode required for accessing storage and services.

In a typical architecture, the gatekeeper pattern acts similarly to a firewall. After analysing the requests, it determines whether to forward them to the host. The gatekeeper validates and sanitizes request content before transmitting it to the host, boosting security by regulating and reducing potential risks and exposures.

You can use this pattern when you are building applications that handle sensitive information, provide services that require a high level of protection against malicious attacks, or execute mission-critical operations that require continuous functionality.

The valet key pattern

The difficulty of granting brief, restricted access to particular resources or services without disclosing primary credentials is addressed by the valet key pattern. This pattern gets its name from the real-world idea of a valet key, in which a car owner

FIGURE 9.4 Gatekeeper pattern

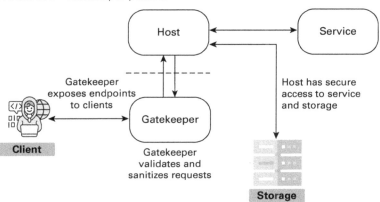

gives a limited-use key to a valet for parking, providing access to the inside while restricting access to the glove compartment and other secure locations.

The valet key pattern is used to improve security and access management. The core idea is to create short-lived and tightly scoped access tokens or keys that offer temporary access for a specified function. By doing so, the primary credentials are protected and access is limited to what is required, reducing the danger associated with extended or broad access.

One of the primary benefits of the valet key pattern is that it can be used in cases where other entities, third-party services or system components require access to specific functionality. Instead of exposing the primary credentials, which may have elevated access, a valet key with carefully defined permissions and a time limit is supplied. This temporary access token enables the entity to carry out the essential tasks without jeopardizing the system's overall security posture.

Implementing the valet key pattern requires careful management of access rules, authentication systems and the production and validation of temporary access tokens. These tokens are set to expire after a predetermined time period or to become invalid

FIGURE 9.5   Valet key pattern

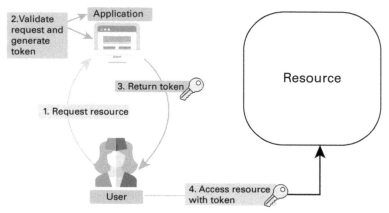

after a specific task. This approach to access management follows the principle of least privilege, ensuring that identities have access only for the duration and scope required to accomplish their specific roles.

The federated identity pattern

The federated identity pattern is a design principle and authentication mechanism that allows users to use a single set of credentials to access many apps or services across multiple domains.

In a federated identity system, a user's identity and authentication information are stored and managed by an identity provider (IdP), which could be entities like Google, Microsoft, or Facebook. When the user attempts to access a service or application in a different domain, the relying party (RP) transfers the authentication process to the identity provider. The user is redirected to the IdP's authentication service, where they provide their credentials. Once authenticated, the IdP generates a security token, often in the form of a security assertion markup language (SAML) token or JSON Web Token (JWT), containing information about the user and their authentication. This token serves as a proof of the user's identity and is then presented to the relying party, allowing the user access to the requested service or application without the need for the RP to directly manage the user's credentials.

'LOGIN WITH GOOGLE' AS AN EXAMPLE OF FEDERATED IDENTITY

'Login with Google' is an example of federated identity login that many of us frequently use. Let's imagine you have a website called learntheadoralanguage.com, and to access its features users need to log in. In this scenario, when a user clicks on 'Login with Google', the process begins by redirecting them to Google to perform the authentication. Google serves as the IdP in this federated identity setup. The user is prompted to enter their Google username and password directly on Google's authentication page. Once the user successfully logs in, Google generates a security token, often in the form of an OAuth token or OpenID Connect ID token. This token contains information about the user and their authenticated status. Subsequently, the user is redirected back to learntheadoralanguage.com with this token. The RP, in this case learntheadoralanguage.com, can trust the authentication performed by Google and use the information in the token to establish a local session for the user. This seamless and secure process enables users to access learntheadoralanguage.com without the need to create and manage separate credentials for the website, demonstrating the federated identity model.

The federated identity pattern has various benefits which have contributed to its widespread use in modern authentication systems. This pattern introduced single sign-on (SSO), in which users authenticate themselves once with the identity provider (such as Google or Microsoft) and get access to different services or apps without repeated logins. This improves user convenience while simultaneously lowering the likelihood of password-related security vulnerabilities. Federated identification also enables centralized identity management via the IdP, which ensures that there is uniform enforcement of security standards, easier administration and quick access updates or revocations across all federated apps. This centralization enables administrators to handle user identities collectively from a single place and this improves consistency and security. Another advantage of the federated identity pattern is that it promotes interoperability and collaboration among many systems and domains. Users from several organizations can work effortlessly, accessing common resources without the difficulty of keeping different identities for each domain, and this is useful in cross-organizational collaborations and partnerships.

REVIEW

In this chapter, we explored the dynamic landscape of cloud security and privacy, as well as the significant issues that come with securing the cloud environment. We went into the difficulties of protecting data and systems in the cloud, addressing crucial concerns such as unauthorized access, data breaches and compliance.

The chapter addressed best practices for strengthening cloud security, covering a wide range of methods like access control, threat modelling, DevSecOps, encryption and incident response. Understanding these practices provided you with insights into developing a strong security posture that ensures the confidentiality, integrity and availability of data in the cloud.

We also looked into cloud security architectural patterns including gatekeeper, valet key and federated identity. These patterns provide a framework for creating secure and resilient cloud systems, as well as strategic solutions to complex security concerns.

As you finish this chapter, you should have a foundational understanding of the complexities of cloud security and privacy. You are more equipped to handle the complexities of safeguarding information in the cloud if you are familiar with the obstacles, best practices and architectural patterns. This contributes to a more secure and resilient cloud ecosystem.

GLOSSARY

ADVANCED ENCRYPTION STANDARD (AES): A widely adopted encryption algorithm known for its efficiency and versatility in securing data at rest and in transit.

API KEY: A unique identifier used to authenticate requests made to a service, allowing secure access to its functionalities.

BLOWFISH: A symmetric-key block cipher known for its simplicity and effectiveness.

CHACHA20: A symmetric encryption algorithm notable for its speed and security.

CIPHERTEXT: The transformed message, appearing as a seemingly random sequence of characters after encryption, rendering it incomprehensible to unauthorized individuals.

CLOUD SECURITY: The practice of protecting data, applications and infrastructure in cloud environments to ensure confidentiality, integrity and availability.

COMMIT HISTORY: A chronological record of changes made to a code repository, providing insights into the development process.

COMPLIANCE: Adherence to specific regulations, standards or legal requirements related to data handling and storage.

CYBER KILL CHAIN: A model describing the stages of a cyber attack, from initial reconnaissance to data exfiltration.

DATA BREACHES: Unintended incidents where unauthorized individuals gain access to sensitive data, leading to potential misuse or exposure.

DATA LOSS: The accidental or intentional removal of crucial data, leading to its permanent absence and potential consequences for an organization.

DECRYPTION: The process of reversing encryption, converting ciphertext back into the original plaintext using the appropriate decryption key.

DEVSECOPS: A contraction of development, security and operations, DevSecOps signifies the integration of security practices throughout the software development life cycle, automating security measures from initial design to deployment.

DIFFIE-HELLMAN KEY EXCHANGE: A method for secure exchange of cryptographic keys over a potentially insecure communication channel.

DISTRIBUTED DENIAL OF SERVICE (DDOS) ATTACKS: Coordinated efforts to overwhelm a target system, network, or application with traffic, disrupting its availability.

DREAD:

DAMAGE: Potential harm resulting from a threat.

REPRODUCIBILITY: The likelihood of the threat being repeatable.

EXPLOITABILITY: The ease with which a threat can be exploited.

AFFECTED USERS: The number of users impacted by the threat.

DISCOVERABILITY: How easily the threat can be discovered.

ELLIPTIC-CURVE CRYPTOGRAPHY (ECC): An asymmetric encryption algorithm specializing in secure communications and key exchange.

ENCRYPTION ALGORITHM: A sophisticated mathematical procedures used to encrypt and decrypt data.

FEDERATED IDENTITY PATTERN: A design principle and authentication mechanism allowing users to use a single set of credentials to access multiple apps or services across various domains.

GATEKEEPER PATTERN: A security pattern used in cloud services to separate the code responsible for public endpoints from the code handling requests and storage access.

HASH FUNCTIONS (E.G. SHA-256): Algorithms that produce fixed-size output (hash) from input data, commonly used for data integrity verification.

HOST AND APPLICATION RISK ANALYSIS (HARA): An analysis method focusing on risks associated with hosts and applications.

IDENTITY AND ACCESS MANAGEMENT (IAM): The practice of ensuring that individuals or systems have the appropriate access to resources in a secure and controlled manner.

INCIDENT RESPONSE: A structured approach to addressing and managing the aftermath of a security breach or incident.

INSECURE COMMIT HISTORY: A security challenge arising from exposing sensitive information, like passwords or keys, in the commit history, making it accessible to unauthorized entities.

IRREGULAR KEY ROTATION: A security challenge stemming from infrequent or inconsistent key rotation practices, potentially leading to vulnerabilities.

JUST-IN-TIME (JIT) ACCESS: Allowing access to resources only when required for a specific task or period, reducing the risk window.

KEY ROTATION: The practice of regularly changing cryptographic keys to enhance security and reduce the risk of unauthorized access.

MULTI-FACTOR AUTHENTICATION (MFA): A security measure requiring users to provide multiple forms of identification before accessing resources.

OPERATIONALLY CRITICAL THREAT, ASSET AND VULNERABILITY EVALUATION (OCTAVE): A risk assessment framework concentrating on operational risk management.

OWASP APPLICATION THREAT MODELLING (OWTF): An approach by the Open Web Application Security Project for identifying and mitigating security risks in applications.

PLAINTEXT: The original, understandable message before undergoing encryption.

PRETTY GOOD PRIVACY (PGP): A hybrid encryption solution combining symmetric and asymmetric cryptography for secure communication.

PRINCIPLE OF LEAST PRIVILEGE (POLP): A security concept advocating that identities should have the minimum necessary access or permissions for their tasks.

PRIVILEGE ESCALATION: The unauthorized elevation of access privileges, allowing an identity to have more extensive control than intended.

PROCESS FOR ATTACK SIMULATION AND THREAT ANALYSIS (PASTA): A comprehensive approach to analysing and simulating potential attacks.

QUALITY ASSURANCE (QA): A systematic process to ensure that software meets specified requirements and standards before release.

RIVEST-SHAMIR-ADLEMAN (RSA): An asymmetric encryption algorithm crucial for secure communications and key exchange processes.

ROLE-BASED ACCESS CONTROL (RBAC): Managing access permissions based on users' roles or functions within an organization.

SOFTWARE DEVELOPMENT LIFE CYCLE (SDLC): The process of designing, developing, testing and deploying software, typically divided into phases to manage the entire development process.

STRIDE:

SPOOFING: Unauthorized entities pretending to be legitimate.

TAMPERING: Unauthorized modification of data or systems.

REPUDIATION: Denying actions, making it difficult to trace.

INFORMATION DISCLOSURE: Unauthorized access to sensitive information.

DENIAL OF SERVICE (DOS): Disruption of services to legitimate users.

ELEVATION OF PRIVILEGE: Unauthorized escalation of user privileges.

THREAT AND RISK INTELLIGENCE KNOWLEDGEBASE (TRIKE): A knowledge base providing a structured approach to threat and risk intelligence.

TRIPLE DES (3DES): An encryption algorithm applying the Data Encryption Standard (DES) cipher three times for increased security.

TWOFISH: A symmetric-key block cipher designed as an improvement to the Blowfish algorithm.

VALET KEY PATTERN: A security pattern addressing the challenge of granting brief, restricted access to specific resources without disclosing primary credentials.

VISUAL, AGILE AND SIMPLE THREAT MODELLING (VAST): A threat modelling framework emphasizing visual and agile methods for simplicity.

## CHAPTER TEN

Migrating to a new cloud provider

In your project or business, you may want to move applications and data from an on-premises server to the cloud, or from one cloud provider to another. This process, known as cloud migration, is good for organizations seeking increased scalability, cost effectiveness and agility that their current solution doesn't give to them in today's volatile business environment. Understanding the complexities of cloud migration is critical for a successful move, whatever your motivation is. In this chapter, we will explore cloud migration, exploring its different types, planning considerations, organizational problems and the tools and technology that expedite the migration process.

Overview of cloud migration

Cloud migration is the process of migrating data, apps and workloads from an on-premises data centre to a cloud-based architecture or from one cloud environment to another. This strategic initiative entails seamlessly transferring digital assets, frequently with the goal of leveraging the cloud provider benefits such as scalability, accessibility and cost-efficiency. To guarantee a smooth transition, the process includes rigorous planning, an assessment of current systems and the implementation of appropriate migration procedures.

Why is cloud migration important?

There are multiple reasons why moving from either on-premises infrastructure or a previous cloud provider is crucial and I'd like to share a few of them:

- *Scalability and flexibility:* When moving from on-premises infrastructure, cloud migration allows businesses to scale their resources up or down based on demand. This scalability provides good performance during peak periods and cost savings during quiet periods.
- *Cost efficiency:* You may optimize workloads for cost in the cloud and there are also huge reductions in equipment, maintenance and real estate expenses.
- *Global accessibility:* Cloud infrastructure provides the advantage of global accessibility, enabling teams to deploy applications and store data in different data centres across the world. This makes it possible for their customers to have a good experience when they try to access data and applications from anywhere with an internet connection. This is especially valuable as work becomes increasingly mobile and remote.
- *Innovation and agility:* Cloud services provide a variety of innovative tools and services that can help businesses run more efficiently. Beyond compute and data storage, cloud providers have services for AI, IoT, governance, augmented/virtual reality, security, media and more. Migrating to the cloud helps organizations to immediately leverage these tools and build more innovative applications on the cloud.

- *Data security and compliance:* Reputable cloud service providers invest significantly in security measures, often outperforming individual organizations' capabilities. Migrating to the cloud provides businesses with cutting-edge security processes while also ensuring compliance with industry requirements.

If you are already on the cloud and you're planning to migrate to a different cloud, it could be because you want to:

- *Optimize costs:* Evaluating and selecting a cloud provider based on your specific needs and pricing structures might result in significant savings. Cloud providers have different pricing schemes and choosing one that matches your budget helps with cost savings. Some providers may provide better pricing for specific workloads or services and organizations might decide to move to take advantage of these cost savings.
- *Enhance performance:* Different cloud providers may offer varying performance capabilities. Migrating to a new provider could be driven by a desire for improved speed, reliability, or overall performance. For example, if a company is experiencing latency issues or wants more processing capacity, switching to a cloud provider with better-suited infrastructure can improve overall application and service performance.
- *Access different services:* Each cloud provider offers a unique collection of services and features. The need to access specific features or services that better align with your product may motivate you to migrate to a different cloud. For example, if a company wishes to leverage advanced machine learning capabilities it may shift to a cloud provider known for its artificial intelligence capabilities.

Types of cloud migration

When thinking about classifying cloud migration, there are two things that are considered: the type of resource being migrated, and the location it is being migrated to. In this section, we will go over the four major types of cloud migration

Data centre migration

Data centre migration is the process of moving data from on-premises servers and mainframes, which are often housed in a server room at a company's headquarters, to servers hosted by a cloud provider. Usually, these cloud servers are located in large, extremely secure and well-maintained data centres.

Usually, organizations use high-capacity networks to send the application, data and other resources on the server to the new cloud platform. Doing this transmission over a high-capacity network can be really efficient and stable. However, when a robust network infrastructure is unavailable or unfeasible, an alternative strategy is used. This involves transferring the data on discs known as 'data boxes'. Once loaded with the necessary data, these data boxes are physically transferred to the specified cloud provider's facility. When the data arrives, it is uploaded to the cloud provider's servers.

This dual strategy, which combines network-based migration and physical data box transfer, guarantees flexibility and adaptability in the face of fluctuating infrastructure restrictions. It enables organizations to overcome network constraints and carry out data centre migrations with efficiency and dependability, hence contributing to the smooth integration of on-premises data into the cloud environment.

Hybrid cloud migration

This involves transferring some resources to the public cloud while keeping others in on-premises data centres. The hybrid cloud scenario allows organizations to capitalize on current on-premises infrastructure investments while also reaping the flexibility, efficiency, strategic value and other benefits of the public cloud.

Hybrid cloud migration is particularly useful for data backup. In this scenario, a company deliberately backs up its private cloud resources on a public cloud. This is a precautionary measure in the event of an unforeseen event that leaves an on-premises data centre useless. Organizations improve their resilience and assure the continuity of vital operations even in the face of unanticipated obstacles by using the public cloud as a secure and off-site backup.

Beyond equipment optimization, the hybrid cloud model enables organizations, particularly those in certain industries, to more easily fulfil industry-specific and governmental compliance needs. Industries with rigorous standards of regulation, such as banking or healthcare, can benefit from hybrid cloud flexibility, allowing them to overcome compliance problems while leveraging the scalability and agility provided by cloud resources. This strategy delivers a tailored solution that meets regulatory requirements without compromising on the strategic advantages of cloud technology.

Cloud-to-cloud migration

Now that cloud computing is ubiquitous, many organizations may use multiple clouds as a result of mergers, acquisitions or the decision to diversify cloud service providers. When operating a multicloud environment, organizations frequently find that it is advantageous to move resources seamlessly across public clouds via a process known as cloud-to-cloud migration. This type of migration is useful when organizations want to take advantage of the diverse products, services and pricing structures provided by different cloud platforms.

Cloud-to-cloud migration enables businesses to optimize their cloud strategy by using the strengths and specialities of different cloud providers. For example, one cloud provider may excel in providing powerful data analytics tools, but another may be known for its high-performance computing skills. These businesses can dynamically assign resources to meet with their developing needs and capitalize on the specific characteristics of each cloud provider within their portfolio by simplifying the transfer of workloads and data between clouds.

Workload-specific migration

Another strategy for cloud migration is to move specific workloads to the cloud. In this scenario, organizations analyse their existing infrastructure strategically and identify key components, such as databases or mainframes, that could benefit from cloud migration. This targeted migration strategy is motivated by a number of factors including the desire for cost savings, increased performance, enhanced security and other attractive benefits associated with cloud environments.

For example, an organization may choose to migrate its databases to the cloud in order to leverage the cloud provider's specialized database services, providing improved data scalability, dependability and management. Moving mainframes to the cloud, on the other hand, can result in cheaper operational expenses, more agility and improved accessibility. Cloud environments also provide enhanced security features, making them a good alternative for organizations looking to improve the security of sensitive data.

By migrating certain workloads, you can enjoy the benefits of cloud computing in a targeted manner, matching your migration efforts with the unique demands and objectives of your business (or project).

Strategies for cloud migration

Success in a cloud migration requires thorough and focused preparation, just like the rigorous planning you put into your personal endeavours. It's similar to planning a major event or an exciting project; you need a well-thought-out strategy that not only outlines your target but also addresses any roadblocks along the way.

If you were organizing a large event, you wouldn't go into it blindly, would you? Similarly, success in cloud migration is dependent on developing a complete strategy. This strategy not only sets the stage for the migration with well-defined goals, but it also serves as a proactive guide, anticipating and addressing any difficulties that may occur along the way.

The migration strategy must include roadmaps, timelines, project metrics and targets. It should also include a communication strategy for informing team leaders, engaging with cloud vendors and keeping other stakeholders informed. Although specific processes may vary depending on a company (or team) and cloud service requirements, this section will cover some cloud migration strategies that can simplify and improve the whole process.

Rehosting

Rehosting, often known as 'lift and shift', is the process of moving an application to a cloud provider's data centre with few changes. This strategy tries to migrate the application effortlessly, preserving the programme's existing functions for everyone while making no visible modifications. The fundamental difference is the transition from an on-premises data centre to a cloud data centre, which is now managed by the provider rather than the organization's internal IT team. This enables the application to benefit from improved infrastructure without requiring significant changes to its core functionality, resulting in a seamless and transparent migration experience.

Replatforming

Replatforming entails moving an on-premises application to the infrastructure of a cloud provider, but with one important difference: it includes upgrades to take advantage of new technologies or services supplied by the cloud service. Unlike a simple lift-and-shift, replatforming makes use of the cloud provider's features to improve the application's performance and capabilities. The goal is to optimize the application for the cloud environment, and benefit from the advantages of modern technology provided by the cloud provider.

Repurchasing

Repurchasing substitutes an on-premises application with a cloud-based, provider-created SaaS application that employees access through a browser. For example, if you've been using a licenced, on-premises CRM solution, you might want to migrate to an enterprise CRM cloud service that you pay for via subscription and that is automatically updated with new features multiple times a year. While this may appear to be a straightforward task, mapping the new application's features to the business processes requires time and careful planning.

Refactoring

Refactoring is a process that involves migrating an application to the cloud with the primary purpose of modernizing its design in order to fully utilize the capabilities of cloud-native features. For example, if the monolithic application that has served its purpose for many years has become difficult to modify according to what customers need, refactoring becomes a strategic method in such instances.

The application might be substantially redesigned during refactoring and one common practice is to migrate from a monolithic architecture to a microservices architecture. This restructuring improves the application's agility by making it more easier to design, test and deploy new features.

Refactoring also enables the incorporation of cloud-native capabilities such as in-database analytics. This entails embedding analytical capabilities directly within the database, eliminating the need for moving data across environments. In essence, refactoring is about future-proofing your application, making it adaptive to changing requirements and capable of using the most recent cloud-native innovations.

Retaining

'If it's not broken, don't fix it.' The decision to retain an application in its present on-premises environment is a deliberate and strategic decision that is driven by a detailed assessment of multiple criteria that collectively decide the feasibility and practicability of a cloud migration. This is a comprehensive decision-making process and various factors may contribute to choosing retention over migration.

For example, applications with strong low-latency requirements may prefer an on-premises architecture. Some tasks require real-time responsiveness and the potential latency introduced by the cloud may fall short of the performance benchmarks established by such applications.

Data residency rules are also important in the choice to keep. Organizations bound by legal or compliance regulations dictating the physical location of data may be wary about migrating to a cloud provider's data centre. Navigating the complicated terrain of legal and regulatory regulations is an important component of this decision – which makes sense, because I don't think any business enjoys getting sued.

Another thing that might make your team not see value in a migration is a careful examination of the costs and effort involved in migrating. It could indicate that, at least under the current conditions, the benefits may not outweigh the cost. This could be influenced by a variety of factors, such as the application's complexity, current infrastructure spending, or budget limits.

Regardless of the decision for retaining, it is important to be open to change. Given the constant growth of the cloud, it is advisable to revisit the idea of cloud migration on a regular basis. Cloud providers are increasing their worldwide presence by creating data centres in new regions, introducing innovative strategies that solve data security concerns and improving migration efficiency. Periodic assessments ensure that the decision matches with the expanding environment of cloud capabilities and remains responsive to the organization's changing demands and possibilities.

Retiring

Retiring is a deliberate action that requires a thorough review of the relevance and utility of an on-premises application. This decision is usually motivated by the realization that the application's functionality is either rarely used or has become outdated, rendering it obsolete in the present operating context.

The act of retiring applications during a cloud migration process has numerous advantages. Organizations may achieve considerable efficiency and cost-effectiveness gains by letting go of underutilized or outdated apps. This method is analogous to cleaning a workspace by removing redundancy and ineffective operations that may incur ongoing costs without providing comparable value.

However, retirement is not a hasty process; it takes thorough planning and execution. Before turning off the application, its dependencies with other apps must be identified and taken care of. This ensures a smooth transition that does not interrupt related systems or have unintended repercussions.

Steps for cloud migration

This section will cover the key steps for migrating to the cloud.

Assessment and planning

When beginning a cloud migration, preparation is necessary. This step entails clearly defining the business rationale for the move and thoroughly grasping the current IT landscape. Teams thoroughly evaluate, inventory and categorize apps and data, analyse dependencies and evaluate the security and compliance requirements. Simultaneously, present infrastructure, apps and data are evaluated to determine their potential for cloud transfer. Setting clear goals and expectations, assessing compatibility with the chosen cloud platform and identifying potential migration issues are all essential components of this crucial planning stage.

Choose your target cloud provider

Following a thorough assessment of existing infrastructure and applications, the next stage in cloud migration is to select the cloud service provider you want to migrate to (it can be multiple providers). Different factors like the provider's interoperability with existing apps and data, service options, pricing models and support capabilities influence the decision of what cloud provider(s) to use. Furthermore, data sovereignty, compliance requirements, scalability and the availability of required resources also play an essential role in this decision-making process.

Design the target cloud architecture

The organization and structuring of the cloud environment's apps, data and infrastructure require rigorous planning that encompasses critical elements to facilitate a stable and effective cloud setup. This phase involves designing scalable and robust cloud infrastructures, defining networking and security configurations and identifying the most relevant cloud services and features. During this phase, some considerations include whether to adopt a microservices architecture by splitting services into smaller components, determining efficient methods for system components to send messages and interact, and evaluating the overall architectural layout for optimal performance and scalability. Addressing these questions and considerations is crucial for creating a well-organized and strategically configured cloud environment that aligns seamlessly with the specific objectives and requirements of the migration project.

Data migration

You will plan and execute data migration to the cloud in a stateful service. A stateful service is a computing service or application that maintains the state or status of a user's interactions, transactions or data across multiple requests. To maintain the state of users' interactions, you need a way to store (or persist) data. An example of a stateful service is an online banking application because it stores the state of a user's financial transactions, account balances and recent activities. This allows users to track and review their financial history.

This migration may involve creating infrastructure to hold the data and then transferring databases, files and other essential data your application needs. The software engineering team should ensure the migration process happens in a way that minimizes downtime and guarantees data consistency during the transition.

Strategies for data migration include:

- Data synchronization between on-premises and cloud environments.
- Choosing the appropriate data transfer methods.
- Validating the integrity of transferred data.

Additionally, considerations for data security, encryption and compliance with regulatory requirements are essential for maintaining the confidentiality and integrity of sensitive information throughout the migration process.

Application migration

In this stage of the cloud migration process, the team will transfer applications to the cloud, ensuring they are compatible with the chosen cloud environment. Depending on the selected migration strategy, such as lift-and-shift, replatforming or refactoring, the execution process involves setting up the target cloud environment. This includes provisioning virtual machines, network resources and more, replicating or migrating data to the cloud and deploying and configuring apps in the new cloud infrastructure.

Testing

Once you have successfully migrated your service to the cloud, testing your service to identify any issues before switching traffic to the new service instances on your new cloud is essential. You should consider doing functional testing. This type of testing ensures that all features operate as expected. Performance testing is also crucial as it helps assess responsiveness and scalability, ensuring the cloud infrastructure can handle the anticipated workload efficiently.

The more we connect people to applications through the cloud, the more there are risks of security breaches. As a result, security testing is vital during this phase to identify and rectify vulnerabilities that might pose threats in the live cloud environment.

In addition to running these various tests after the migration, establishing robust observability becomes an ongoing operational necessity. Setting up observability involves tracking logs, metrics and traces creating a proactive monitoring strategy. Observability is essential for the timely detection and resolution of any unforeseen issues that may arise in the live cloud environment. Continuous monitoring ensures that your cloud-deployed service operates optimally, meets performance standards and addresses potential challenges promptly. When you monitor your cloud service, you can eventually catch issues you skipped in your testing phase.

Post-migration support

After testing your cloud migration and setting up monitoring, you should also set up post-migration support. This involves initiating an on-call rotation, which is critical to ensuring your services' ongoing reliability and performance in the cloud environment. An on-call rotation typically consists of a schedule where designated team members take turns being on-call during specified periods, including nights and weekends. During their on-call shifts, team members are responsible for promptly addressing any issues, incidents or emergencies that may arise with the migrated services.

The on-call rotation is a proactive measure to quickly respond to potential issues, minimizing downtime and ensuring a seamless user experience. Team members on-call should have a comprehensive understanding of the migrated infrastructure, applications and the cloud environment, allowing them to troubleshoot, diagnose and resolve issues efficiently. This approach aligns with the principles of DevOps and promotes a culture of continuous improvement and accountability.

Additionally, post-migration support involves regular reviews and evaluations of the system's performance and the effectiveness of incident response. Teams may conduct post-incident reviews to analyse the root causes of any disruptions and implement preventive measures to enhance system resilience. These post-incident reviews can be organized bi-weekly for the people who had on-call shifts during that period, as well as other key stakeholders (e.g. team leads) to come together, discuss the incidents that occurred, take on action items, if any, and learn from the experience. Ongoing training and knowledge sharing within the team contribute to building expertise and refining the support process for sustained success in the cloud environment.

Post-migration documentation

In case a new member joins the team or for future reference, it is crucial to thoroughly document the new architecture and procedures implemented during the migration process. Documentation is valuable for onboarding new team members, ensuring a smooth transition and reducing the learning curve. It provides insights into the complexities of the migrated infrastructure, the rationale behind specific decisions and the overall design philosophy.

Remember that your documentation should evolve as things change, and they inevitably will. Regularly updating documentation is essential for keeping it accurate and relevant, especially as technologies, best practices and configurations can evolve.

Go-live

At this point, you can go live. However, transitioning your users from the previous service to the migrated one should be a carefully orchestrated process so that the user experience isn't profoundly affected. There are several strategies you can employ in this transition phase.

One approach is the 'Big Bang' strategy, where you simultaneously switch all users to the new service. This method is straightforward but may pose challenges if unforeseen issues arise during the transition, potentially impacting all users simultaneously. Doing this might involve updating DNS names to new domain names. However, it would be best if you were very careful here; meticulous planning is essential to minimize the risk of disruptions. It's crucial to thoroughly test the new service in an environment that mirrors the production setup, ensuring all systems function seamlessly before executing the full switch. Additionally, having a rollback plan is an excellent idea if your team needs to return to the previous state or unexpected issues arise during the transition.

Another strategy is the 'phased transition', where you gradually migrate users in stages. This allows you to identify and address any issues on a smaller scale before rolling out the changes to a broader user base. It provides a more controlled transition and minimizes the impact of potential disruptions. One way to implement this strategy is by rolling out changes based on geolocation, focusing on specific regions or user groups at a time. Alternatively, you can prioritize features or user segments, migrating them incrementally to ensure a smooth and manageable transition.

Additionally, you can use the 'parallel operation' strategy, which involves running both the old and new services simultaneously for a designated period. The parallel operation strategy provides a safety net by keeping the existing service operational while testing the new environment. To facilitate this, you can introduce a traffic manager that dynamically routes requests to both services based on priority, with the new service assigned a higher priority. If the new service becomes unreachable, the traffic manager seamlessly redirects traffic to the older, stable service, ensuring continuity of service. During this coexistence period, the team can proactively identify errors in the new service, address

FIGURE 10.1   The parallel operation strategy

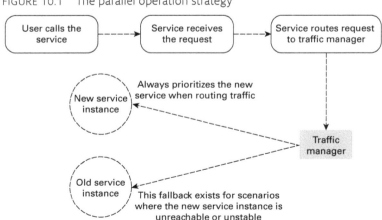

them and perform necessary fixes, all while maintaining operational stability through the fallback mechanism provided by the older service. This approach enhances the overall robustness of the migration process, allowing for iterative improvements and minimizing potential user impact during the transition.

Review and iterate

After successfully migrating to the new cloud service and establishing robust documentation and operations for continuous support, the journey evolves into the 'review and iterate' phase. In this crucial stage, ongoing learning and improvement take centre stage. This involves monitoring key performance indicators, analysing user feedback, conducting security audits, optimizing costs, implementing automated testing, planning for scalability, updating documentation and investing in team training. When there is a culture of continuous improvement, software engineering teams can ensure that their cloud service meets current requirements and remains adaptable to evolving business needs and technological advancements.

REVIEW

In this chapter, you learned about cloud migration and the different types of cloud migration. You also considered the strategies for migrating to a new cloud and the steps to take if you ever want to carry out a cloud migration.

By understanding these concepts, you've equipped yourself with the knowledge needed to make informed decisions, ensuring a well-planned and successful migration that aligns with your organization's specific needs and goals. Whether considering rehosting, replatforming, repurchasing, refactoring, retaining or retiring, you now have a nuanced understanding of how organizations tailor their migration approaches based on distinct circumstances.

GLOSSARY

CLOUD MIGRATION: Seamlessly moving data, applications and workloads from an on-premises data centre to a cloud-based architecture or transferring from one cloud environment to another.

CLOUD-TO-CLOUD MIGRATION: The seamless movement of resources across different public clouds within a multicloud environment, allowing organizations to take advantage of diverse products, services and pricing structures provided by various cloud platforms.

COST EFFICIENCY: The optimization of workloads for cost in the cloud, resulting in reductions in equipment, maintenance and real estate expenses.

DATA CENTRE MIGRATION: Transferring data from on-premises servers and mainframes to servers hosted by a cloud provider, often involving high-capacity networks or physical data box transfers for efficiency and stability.

GLOBAL ACCESSIBILITY: The advantage provided by cloud infrastructure that enables the deployment of applications and storage of data in different data centres worldwide, ensuring accessibility from anywhere with an internet connection.

HYBRID CLOUD MIGRATION: Moving some resources to the public cloud while retaining others in on-premises data centres, balancing leveraging existing infrastructure investments and gaining benefits from the public cloud, such as flexibility, efficiency and strategic value.

REFACTORING: The migration process aimed at modernizing the design of an application to utilize cloud-native features fully. It may involve significant redesign, such as transitioning from a monolithic to a microservices architecture, enhancing agility and incorporating cloud-native capabilities like in-database analytics.

REHOSTING (LIFT-AND-SHIFT): A cloud migration strategy involving the transfer of an application to a cloud provider's data centre with minimal changes, allowing the application to benefit from improved infrastructure without significant modifications to its core functionality.

REPLATFORMING: The process of migrating an on-premises application to a cloud provider's infrastructure, accompanied by upgrades to leverage new technologies or services, optimizing the application for improved performance and capabilities.

REPURCHASING: The strategy of replacing an on-premises application with a cloud-based SaaS application provided by a third party, accessed through a browser.

RETAINING: The deliberate decision to keep an application in its current on-premises environment, driven by factors such as low-latency requirements, data residency rules, cost considerations and the complexity of migration.

RETIRING: The intentional removal of an on-premises application during a cloud migration due to its limited or outdated functionality.

SCALABILITY: The capability of a system to handle an increasing amount of work or its potential to be enlarged to accommodate that growth.

WORKLOAD-SPECIFIC MIGRATION: A strategy focusing on migrating specific workloads to the cloud based on a strategic analysis of existing infrastructure.

## CHAPTER ELEVEN

Cloud cost management

As businesses move to the cloud, keeping things within budget is still important even as the applications scale. This chapter will introduce you to the concept of cloud cost management. As you scale your cloud applications, understanding how to optimize and control costs in the cloud is paramount. Cloud computing offers incredible flexibility and scalability, allowing businesses to adapt to changing demands and innovate rapidly; however, without effective cost management, the cloud's advantages can quickly become financial challenges.

Understanding cloud costs

The cost of cloud computing varies significantly depending on the service and vendor. While most organizations can accurately estimate the expenses of establishing and maintaining their IT infrastructure, many cannot anticipate the costs of transferring their operations to the cloud. This lack of clarity is due to the dynamic and on-demand nature of cloud resources, which can result in fluctuating and difficult-to-predict expenses.

To effectively evaluate, regulate and optimize cloud costs, organizations must take a holistic approach that considers all aspects of their cloud usage. Understanding the many cost-influencing aspects, analysing organizational needs, developing a strategic plan and regularly monitoring and optimizing resource consumption are all part of this process. As an organization, you can also adopt financial operations (FinOps) as part of your overall strategy.

FinOps is a set of strategies that brings together finance, technology and business teams to manage expenses related to cloud computing collaboratively. Its goal is to connect cloud spending with organizational goals, resulting in improved financial visibility and control in the cloud environment. FinOps bridges the gap between technology and finance teams by integrating financial accountability into the day-to-day operations of cloud management.

FinOps involves knowing and auditing cloud spending. Thus, teams must understand how to break down the cost of cloud computing to do so successfully. This means examining the complicated network of charges associated with cloud services to acquire specific insight into how resources are distributed and how they contribute to total spending.

The main components of cloud costs

Typically, the breakdown of cloud computing costs includes several main components. The first consideration is compute cost, which includes costs for virtual machines, containers and any other computational resources needed. A variety of compute instance types are available from most cloud providers, each with a certain capacity for CPU, memory and, occasionally, specialized hardware like graphics acceleration or fast networking. The customer is charged according to the number, type and duration of instances used.

Another component of cloud charges is storage. To make informed decisions about where and how data is stored, teams must understand the specifics of different storage classes, data transport costs and redundancy alternatives. Knowing about data retrieval and deletion costs also contributes to a thorough knowledge of storage costs. Typically, cloud providers have what is called 'storage as a service'. With this, customers pay for elastic storage services by the GB-month of storage used. A GB-month is calculated by averaging the daily peak storage over a billing period (30 days). They can also pay for managed storage services, such as managed disks attached to compute instances. For this, they pay for an entire storage volume, regardless of the amount of storage used on the volume.

Data transfer costs, both within the cloud provider's network and to the internet, also contribute to the overall cost. Teams should also be mindful of data transfer speeds and geographic data distribution, as these aspects can have a substantial impact on expenses.

Aside from these essential components, additional services like load balancing, database usage and network-related charges add to the overall cloud cost. To effectively break down these expenses, engineering and cloud teams must look into service-specific pricing data and consumption trends to discover opportunities for optimization.

To make cloud cost management more streamlined, you should take advantage of cloud cost management tools and services. These tools provide deep insights into spending trends, resource utilization and cost optimization recommendations. They make it possible for teams to visualize cost breakdowns, allocate money to specific projects or departments and implement financial limits.

Cost management tools

There are different cloud cost management solutions organizations may use to gain insights into how they use the cloud and efficiently optimize costs. You can use the tools provided by AWS, Azure, Google, IBM, Oracle and other cloud providers because they are especially built for integrating easily with their individual platforms. These native tools provide extensive visibility into resource utilization, cost breakdowns and performance data, giving you a complete picture of your cloud setup. They frequently include tools such as budgeting, alerting and recommendations to assist you in proactively managing and controlling costs.

You can also use custom tools like Cloudability or Flexera, which offer cross-cloud compatibility. These third-party tools provide a centralized view of your multicloud environment, allowing you to analyse and optimize costs across different cloud providers. They often come with advanced reporting, forecasting and automation features, enabling more granular control over your cloud expenses.

You should consider your organization's unique demands and specifications when determining which tools are appropriate for you and your team. The scope of your cloud deployment, the complexity of your workloads and the level of customization required will all influence your tool selection. Evaluating the user interface, ease of integration and the availability of features such as real-time monitoring and cost allocation capabilities are also critical factors.

By selecting tools that align with your goals, you ensure you have access to reliable and actionable insights to help your team's proactive and long-term cloud cost optimization. Whether you use native cloud provider tools or third-party solutions, the idea is to arm your team with the information they need to make informed decisions, collaborate and ultimately achieve cost-efficiency in your cloud operations.

Cloud cost models

To fully understand cloud costs, you must first learn about the various cloud cost models. This knowledge enables you to make informed decisions when picking infrastructure resources, all while keeping your budget in mind. Cloud cost models give a pricing and invoicing structure, allowing you to optimize spending based on the specific needs of your workloads. There are different cloud cost models that you can combine depending on your needs.

Pay-as-you-go

Pay-as-you-go (PAYG) is a cloud cost model that provides flexibility by billing users based on actual computing resource consumption, usually on an hourly or per-minute basis. This on-demand model eliminates the need for upfront commitments, allowing organizations to scale resources up or down dynamically in response to changing demand. PAYG, which is especially well-suited for fluctuating workloads, enables organizations to easily control expenses while assuring peak performance and scaling down during calmer hours.

For example, if you sell Christmas sweaters, your peak seasons will naturally revolve around the holiday season. A PAYG model would be highly beneficial for managing the variable demand associated with this business. You can smoothly scale up your computing resources as the holiday season approaches to manage increased website traffic, online orders and customer interactions. This adaptability guarantees that your e-commerce platform runs effectively over the Christmas season, giving a great customer experience without the need for costly upfront commitments.

Alternatively, during non-peak times when demand for Christmas sweaters falls, a PAYG approach allows you to scale down your resources, eliminating unnecessary expenses. This versatility guarantees that you only pay for the computing power that you really use, aligning your prices with your business's variable demands.

Reserved instances

Reserved instances (RIs) are a strategic option within cloud cost models that provide enterprises with a path to significant cost savings through commitment and predictability. RIs, in contrast to the on-demand flexibility of PAYG, require a commitment to a specified quantity of cloud resources for a set period, typically one or three years. In exchange for this commitment, cloud providers offer a lower cost than the variable pricing associated with PAYG. This paradigm is ideal for businesses with stable and predictable workloads, where resource requirements remain consistent over time.

The primary benefit of RIs is the significant cost savings they provide over time. Businesses can guarantee a predictable pricing structure and effectively lock in a discounted rate by committing to a defined amount of resources for an extended period. This predictability is especially useful for workloads with stable resource requirements, allowing organizations to optimize their budgeting and distribute funding more efficiently over the reservation term.

Remember your Christmas sweater business? Now imagine if your brand sold other clothes online and you experience a predictable spike during annual sales events like Black Friday. You can strategically use RIs to enhance performance and cost-effectiveness during these peak periods. You can commit to RIs, securing a specific amount of computing resources for a defined term, typically one or three years. This commitment ensures a discounted rate compared to on-demand pricing, providing stability and significant cost savings.

As Black Friday approaches, RIs ensure that your e-commerce platform is dedicated and has guaranteed resources, removing the risk of performance issues or service disruptions due to the predicted increase in customer traffic. The long-term commitment fits in perfectly with the predictable nature of the annual sales spike, allowing your business to cut costs while maintaining high service reliability. This consistency is critical for supporting additional site traffic, order processing and consumer interactions during significant sales events.

The financial predictability of RIs also enables your business to properly manage its budget, deploy resources strategically and avoid unexpected costs associated with variable pricing models. By implementing RIs into your cloud cost strategy, your company can securely navigate Black Friday and other sales occasions, giving customers a seamless and delightful online shopping experience. This planned use of RIs ensures operational stability at peak times and adds to long-term cost-effectiveness.

Spot instances

Spot instances are a flexible and cost-effective cloud cost model. In contrast to the predictable nature of RIs or the on-demand flexibility of PAYG, spot instances incorporate an element of market-driven pricing and short-term availability. This concept allows customers to bid on underutilized cloud capacity, with the potential for significant cost reductions over regular PAYG rates. Organizations can profit from cost-effective computational power by taking advantage of extra resources in the cloud environment during decreased demand.

However, it is essential to realize that the transient nature of spot instances comes with a trade-off. When the reclaimed capacity is needed for on-demand or reserved workloads, the cloud provider can terminate these instances with little warning. As a result, spot instances are ideal for fault-tolerant and flexible workloads that can endure interruptions and react to changes in resource availability.

Spot instances work well for operations that can be distributed and parallelized across numerous instances, such as batch processing, data analysis, or rendering functions. Organizations can considerably cut expenses by using spare capacity during off-peak hours or when overall demand is low. However, it is critical to develop strategies for dealing with disruptions gracefully. This ensures that the organization can leverage the cost advantages of spot instances while maintaining the dependability and resilience required for specific workloads.

Savings plans

Savings plans are a cost-saving strategy provided by some cloud providers, allowing organizations to compromise between the commitment associated with RIs and the adaptability of PAYG models. In the savings plans model, users agree to a consistent quantity of cloud consumption, often measured in dollars per hour ($/hr), for a specified term of one or three years. In exchange for this commitment, cloud providers offer a discount, allowing organizations to save money while keeping the flexibility of PAYG.

Cloud cost management strategies

Cloud cost management strategies help organizations optimize their cloud spending, maximizing their resources while maintaining financial efficiency. These strategies are crucial in aligning cloud expenditures with organizational goals and preventing unnecessary costs. This section will cover some proven strategies for managing your cloud costs, offering insights into how businesses can achieve cost-effectiveness and maximize the value of their cloud investments.

Budget control

Budget control is a foundational pillar for efficient cloud cost management, requiring organizations to act proactively in setting and enforcing financial constraints. As an organization, you should define budgets for your cloud services, matching these financial allocations with the larger goals and priorities of the business. This process comprehensively evaluates anticipated resource needs, performance requirements and strategic objectives to arrive at realistic and well-informed budgetary figures.

The next crucial step after budgets are created is to ensure all relevant teams are aware of and follow them. Teams in charge of various projects or departments must be well-versed in the budget limits related to their initiatives. This transparency develops a responsible culture and empowers teams to make educated resource utilization decisions, highlighting the significance of matching operations with financial restrictions.

Organizations can set up monitoring tools to effectively enforce budget control, enabling real-time visibility of spending patterns. Regular and transparent reporting ensures that teams know their spending and budgets. When a project is approaching or beyond its budget, alerts and notifications can drive remedial steps, preventing potential overruns.

Organizations can also incorporate controls in their cloud service platforms to automatically restrict resource provisioning or to trigger alarms when budget thresholds are approaching. These controls act like safeguards and they help to limit unintentional spending.

Right sizing

Right sizing involves matching the allocated cloud resources to the actual needs and demands of the organization. This method ensures that compute instances, storage volumes and other cloud services are matched to the precise needs of the workload, avoiding wasteful overprovisioning. It is a common challenge in cloud environments to provision resources based on initial estimations or generic configurations, often leading to underutilization and increased costs.

To optimize rightsizing, you should carefully examine the cloud workloads' actual usage patterns and performance needs. By carefully monitoring historical data and resource consumption, your team can discover instances where resources are routinely underutilized. This granular understanding allows teams to make precise adjustments, ensuring each resource is provisioned at the optimal level necessary for efficient operation.

Detecting unused resources

Detecting unused resources is essential because it allows engineering teams to find and eliminate redundant resources within their cloud deployment. Resources like compute instances, storage volumes and load balancers can be provisioned but are not always used. As an engineering team, it's important to proactively analyse your cloud environment for idle resources and remove them from the infrastructure to save expenses and streamline resource allocation.

Compute instances, for example, are usually deployed for testing or other specific tasks but may remain active after they are needed. Storage volumes and snapshots also created for backup or testing purposes can accumulate over time, consuming valuable cloud resources.

It's essential to implement tools or scripts that regularly scan the cloud deployment for unused resources – you can set a cron job, which is a unit of work that runs periodically. These tools can analyse metadata, utilization metrics and activity logs to identify resources that have been dormant or underutilized for extended periods. Once identified, your team can take corrective action by terminating, archiving or appropriately resizing these resources.

Autoscaling

Autoscaling is a flexible solution that adapts to the changing demands of applications and workloads. This strategy enables organizations to manage their cloud resources more efficiently by dynamically altering the scale of computing instances, storage and other services based on real-time application demand. Autoscaling's primary goal is to ensure that the infrastructure is ideally matched with the shifting needs of the application, increasing both performance efficiency and cost-effectiveness.

Autoscaling enables organizations to scale resources up during periods of heightened demand, such as peak usage times or sudden traffic spikes, and scale down when there is low traffic. This dynamic adjustment ensures that the organization only pays for the additional cloud resources required to meet the surge in demand, avoiding unnecessary costs associated with the continuous maintenance of high-capacity infrastructure.

Scheduling

Scheduling allows organizations to reduce costs by matching the availability of cloud services to actual usage patterns. Many cloud services are not required to run continuously and teams can shut down these services during inactivity by establishing scheduling protocols. This strategy ensures that resources are only activated when needed, significantly reducing costs while preserving operational efficiency.

Consider the following scenario: a team in Lagos, Nigeria collaborates using cloud services. Outside of usual Lagos business hours, various services, such as development environments, databases or testing environments, may not be required. The team can manage the automatic shutdown of these services during non-business hours by exploiting scheduling capabilities, effectively halting resource usage and minimizing expenses during periods of reduced demand.

A development environment the Lagos team uses for coding and testing can be designed to shut down at night and weekends. This ensures that computing resources are turned off while the development team is not actively working. As a result, the organization saves money on cloud resources that would otherwise be idle during non-operational periods.

This scheduling strategy is helpful for global teams working across different time zones. It allows for the customization of resource availability based on the working hours of specific teams, optimizing cloud spending without compromising accessibility during active operational periods.

REVIEW

In this chapter, you learned about cloud cost management. This knowledge is valuable for organizations or engineering teams aiming to optimize their cloud infrastructure and operate within budget constraints. Understanding cloud cost management empowers you to make informed decisions, strategically allocate resources and ensure cost-effectiveness throughout the life cycle of your cloud services. This chapter covered FinOps, cloud cost components, cost management tools, cloud cost models and some cost management strategies.

These insights will give you a valuable headstart as you continue building cloud services. However, there's much more to discover and refine as you navigate the complexities of cloud economics, adapt to changing workloads and harness the full potential of the cloud. The knowledge gained in this chapter will allow you to manage cloud costs more effectively and make well-informed decisions to drive success as you build on the cloud.

GLOSSARY

CLOUD COMPUTING COSTS: The expenses associated with utilizing cloud services, including compute resources, storage, data transfer and additional services, incurred by organizations or individuals based on their usage.

CLOUD COST MANAGEMENT TOOLS: Tools and services designed to streamline and enhance the management of cloud costs, offering insights into spending trends, resource utilization and optimization recommendations.

FINANCIAL OPERATIONS (FINOPS): A collaborative approach that integrates finance, technology and business teams to manage cloud-related expenses effectively, aligning spending with organizational goals.

PAY-AS-YOU-GO (PAYG): A cloud cost model where users are billed based on actual computing resource consumption, typically on an hourly or per-minute basis.

RESERVED INSTANCES (RIS): A cloud cost model that requires a commitment to a specified quantity of cloud resources for a set period.

RESOURCE UTILIZATION: The effective use of cloud resources, considering factors such as peak usage, consumption trends and opportunities for optimization to maximize efficiency and cost-effectiveness.

RIGHT SIZING: Right sizing in cloud computing is optimizing allocated resources to precisely match a workload's actual needs and demands, maximizing performance and cost-effectiveness.

SPOT INSTANCES: A cloud cost model that allows users to bid on underutilized cloud capacity, potentially offering significant cost reductions. Ideal for fault-tolerant and flexible workloads but comes with the risk of termination with little warning.

## CHAPTER TWELVE

Navigating cloud careers

A cloud profession requires a combination of technical expertise, agility and strategic decision-making. Professionals in
this industry are at the forefront of innovation, influencing the
digital infrastructure of organizations across industries as more
and more businesses adopt cloud technologies. This chapter
introduces you to different job roles in cloud computing, spot-
lighting the diverse opportunities available and providing
insights on how you can strategically navigate them.

Cloud computing roles

A cloud computing role requires you to work in the context of the
cloud. In these roles, you'll collaborate with cross-functional
teams, ensuring seamless integration of applications and services
into the cloud. These roles span a range of responsibilities, e.g.
designing scalable architectures, building and deploying services,
providing robust security measures and more. Here are some key
cloud computing job roles and their respective responsibilities.

Cloud software architect

A cloud architect is responsible for a company's cloud computing system. They work with cloud technology to create cloud adoption plans, cloud application design and cloud management, monitoring and maintenance systems. A solid experience in computer operating systems, programming languages, networking and security is required to become a cloud architect.

A software architect is typically an advanced role that is a natural progression for someone with extensive engineering experience. This role is the product of years of technical knowledge in software development and cloud technologies. Software architects use their extensive programming knowledge, design patterns and application life cycle management to create sophisticated software solutions for cloud settings. Their responsibilities include optimizing individual software applications and strategically aligning architectures with overall corporate goals.

DevOps engineer

The primary duty of a DevOps engineer is to automate and streamline operations ranging from code development and testing to deployment and maintenance. Continuous integration and continuous deployment (CI/CD), infrastructure as code (IaC) and automation are practices used by DevOps engineers to accelerate software delivery while retaining stability and quality. They work with development teams to easily integrate code changes, ensuring that applications can be released quickly and consistently. DevOps engineers collaborate with operations teams to automate infrastructure provisioning, manage configurations and monitor system performance simultaneously. This position promotes culture change by increasing collaboration, communication and shared accountability within the development and operations teams.

A DevOps engineer should be proficient in scripting and programming languages (e.g. Python, Bash), proficient in IaC and configuration management tools (e.g. Terraform, Ansible, Puppet), familiar with CI/CD tools (e.g. Jenkins, GitLab CI) and knowledgeable about containerization and orchestration tools such as Docker and Kubernetes. DevOps engineers should also be familiar with version control systems (e.g. Git), have prior expertise with cloud platforms (e.g. AWS, Azure) and have good problem-solving and collaborative skills.

Site reliability engineer

A site reliability engineer (SRE) maintains the reliability, performance and scalability of an organization's software systems and applications. SREs integrate aspects of software engineering and operations to produce robust, scalable and efficient systems. Their primary objective is to automate and optimize operations to prevent and mitigate system faults. SREs seek to improve a system's overall reliability by adopting monitoring solutions, doing performance analysis and responding to incidents as soon as possible. They work closely with development teams to influence application architecture and design, ensuring they are dependable and resilient. SREs are also critical in capacity planning, risk assessment and balancing system stability and feature development.

A solid experience in software engineering, competency in programming languages (e.g. Python, C#, Java), expertise in system administration and troubleshooting and an in-depth knowledge of distributed systems and network architecture are all required for a site reliability engineer. SREs should be comfortable with automation tools like Ansible or Terraform, containerization technologies like Docker and orchestration tools like Kubernetes. Strong cooperation and communication skills are also required, as SREs frequently collaborate across teams to apply reliability best practices and contribute to a culture of continuous improvement. A SRE must be able to analyse and respond to incidents quickly and be proactive in preventing future problems.

Cloud security specialist/engineer

As more applications move to the cloud, security in the cloud is becoming increasingly important and needs to be prioritized. A cloud security engineer ensures an organization's cloud infrastructure is secure against potential attacks and vulnerabilities. This work entails implementing robust security measures to safeguard sensitive data, apps and systems hosted in the cloud. The cloud security engineer incorporates security best practices into the design and deployment of cloud-based solutions while working with the engineering teams. To protect against cyber threats, unauthorized access and data breaches, they do detailed risk assessments, identify vulnerabilities and implement security controls. Cloud security engineers must also be current with emerging security risks and compliance requirements specific to cloud environments. These people are important in ensuring a safe and compliant cloud architecture.

A deep understanding of cloud platforms, expertise in cloud security principles and best practices, and proficiency in security technologies such as identity and access management (IAM), encryption and security information and event management (SIEM) systems are essential for a cloud security engineer. Being familiar with compliance requirements such as GDPR, HIPAA and industry-specific regulations is also critical. Cloud security engineers should be capable of conducting security audits, establishing security automation and responding quickly to security issues. Effective communication and teamwork skills are also required as they collaborate across teams to advocate for security measures and guarantee an organization-wide approach to cloud security.

Cloud solutions architect

For a lot of organizations, this role means different things across the industry. This is due to the fact that there are different types of solution architects. In some companies they are very technical, while in other companies they are more business consulting focused. However, solutions architects primarily create, optimize and maintain cloud computing solutions for clients. This is different from a software architect, who is focused on the architecture of the internal cloud infrastructure. Clients are usually integrating your solution and building on top of your cloud service, so solutions architects help guide them in structuring their applications effectively within the cloud environment. They collaborate closely with clients to understand their unique requirements, designing end-to-end solutions that encompass various cloud services, infrastructure components, security measures and compliance standards. In essence, cloud solutions architects act as the bridge between clients and the cloud platform, ensuring that the implemented solutions not only meet the technical specifications but also align seamlessly with the clients' business objectives, scalability needs and operational efficiency.

Cloud software engineer

A cloud software engineer builds software applications that leverage the cloud. These applications are called cloud services. Cloud services include Azure CosmosDB (database), Amazon S3 (object storage), NVIDIA GeForce NOW (cloud gaming) and more.

As a cloud software engineer, you should have a diverse set of skills to be able to develop, test and deploy cloud-based applications. To effectively manage the difficulties of cloud computing, you should have various skills as a cloud software developer. First, a solid foundation in programming languages such as Python, Java or C# is required because it serves as a basis for developing and managing cloud applications. Understanding cloud platforms such as AWS, Azure and Google Cloud is critical, as is understanding their individual services, infrastructure and deployment models.

Cloud software engineers work on the design and implementation of scalable and resilient architectures. This involves using cloud-native development approaches such as microservices architecture, containerization with tools such as Docker and Kubernetes and serverless computing with platforms such as AWS Lambda and Azure Functions. Building feature-rich cloud apps requires proficiency in accessing cloud services and APIs for diverse functionalities such as storage, database administration and machine learning. CI/CD practices are also important for engineers to automate the development and deployment processes.

Cloud support engineer

I've seen a few job roles recently where this role was called 'cloud customer engineer' in some companies. However, a cloud support engineer's primary responsibility is to provide technical assistance and support to customers using cloud services. This includes answering questions, diagnosing problems and advising customers to effectively utilize cloud platforms such as AWS, Azure, or Google Cloud. Cloud support engineers play an important role in delivering a great customer experience by resolving technical issues, offering solutions and providing insights into cloud infrastructure optimization.

Some skills you should have as a cloud support engineer centre around a thorough understanding of cloud technologies. It's important to know cloud platforms and you should also have good problem-solving and communication skills. The ability to diagnose and fix problems coupled with a customer-centric attitude are critical for successful interactions with clients. For some companies, cloud support engineers might also need to be comfortable with scripting languages, understand networking fundamentals and have experience with monitoring and debugging tools.

Cloud infrastructure engineer

A cloud infrastructure engineer focuses on designing, implementing and managing the infrastructure components for cloud environments. Unlike traditional infrastructure engineers, those working on the cloud usually leverage the capabilities of cloud service providers such as AWS, Azure, Google Cloud, or others. Their role involves optimizing and maintaining cloud-based resources, ensuring scalability, efficiency and security in alignment with an organization's goals. They are proficient at using IaC tools like Azure Bicep, CloudFormation or Terraform to automate the provisioning and management of cloud resources.

Platform engineer

Platform engineering is an evolving part of the cloud computing and DevOps ecosystem. A platform engineer is responsible for designing, building and maintaining the fundamental platform that enables application development and deployment within an organization. This platform often contains the tools, services and infrastructure required to optimize the software development life cycle while maintaining efficiency, scalability and stability.

Platform engineers work at the intersection of development and operations, collaborating with software developers, system administrators and other stakeholders to create a seamless and automated platform. They leverage DevOps principles to implement IaC, containerization and orchestration technologies to enhance the deployment and management of applications. The goal is to provide a standardized and self-service platform enabling development teams to build, test and deploy applications quickly and consistently. This self-service platform is typically called the internal developer platform.

System administrator

A sysadmin, short for system administrator, manages and maintains the operational health of an organization's computer systems and networks. They ensure that the infrastructure runs smoothly, securely and efficiently. Sysadmins handle various tasks, including server configuration, network administration, system monitoring, troubleshooting and security management. They are also responsible for setting up, configuring and maintaining servers and other computing systems. They manage user accounts, permissions and access controls, ensuring that the organization's data is secure and accessible only to authorized individuals.

In addition, sysadmins implement and oversee backup and recovery processes to safeguard against data loss. Due to the integration of cloud technologies, modern sysadmins often work with cloud platforms, configuring and managing virtual machines, containers and other cloud-based services. They are also usually involved in automating routine tasks using scripting languages or configuration management tools to enhance efficiency and reduce manual work.

Networking engineer

A cloud networking engineer designs, implements and manages networking solutions within cloud environments. Unlike traditional networking engineers, a cloud networking engineer's expertise extends to cloud platforms. Their role involves architecting and optimizing network infrastructure to support the deployment of applications and services in the cloud.

Some tasks that cloud networking engineers do include configuring virtual networks, subnets and routing tables while also ensuring connectivity between various cloud resources. To create a resilient and high-performance network foundation, they work with cloud-specific networking services like Amazon VPC, Azure Virtual Network, Google VPC and more.

Cloud sales specialist

Engineering disciplines are great, but selling to customers makes businesses profitable at the end of the day. To sell cloud computing solutions, organizations hire people to fill cloud sales specialist roles. A cloud sales specialist promotes and sells cloud services to businesses. In this role, cloud sales specialists should understand cloud technologies and be able to communicate the advantages of cloud solutions to potential clients. Working for cloud service providers or technology companies, cloud sales specialists play a critical role in driving revenue by acquiring new customers and expanding the adoption of cloud services within existing accounts.

The responsibilities of a cloud sales specialist include prospecting and identifying potential clients, understanding their specific business needs and presenting cloud solutions that address those needs effectively. Successful cloud sales specialists collaborate closely with clients so that they can gain a deep understanding of their existing infrastructure, business objectives and challenges. By aligning cloud services with these factors, they can optimize operations and contribute to the overall success of the client's business.

Technical product manager

In the context of the cloud, a technical product manager is responsible for overseeing the development and management of cloud-based products within a technology company. This role combines cloud expertise with product management skills.

The key responsibilities of a technical product manager include collaborating with teams, such as engineering, marketing and sales, to define the product roadmap and strategy. They work closely with software developers to ensure that the technical aspects of the cloud product align with the company's goals and meet customer needs. In addition to technical knowledge, project management and communication skills are essential for technical product managers.

They must effectively communicate the product vision, features and benefits to technical and non-technical stakeholders and they also play a crucial role in prioritizing features, managing product releases and ensuring that the engineering team delivers high-quality products on schedule.

Documentation engineer

A documentation engineer (in the context of the cloud) creates, maintains and improves documentation related to cloud technologies and services. This role ensures that users, developers and other stakeholders can access accurate, comprehensive and up-to-date documentation to implement cloud solutions effectively. Technical documentation includes a wide range of materials such as user guides, API documentation, tutorials, troubleshooting guides and best practice documents.

FinOps specialist

A FinOps (financial operations) specialist's primary role is to ensure the successful management and optimization of an organization's cloud spending. FinOps specialists closely monitor and evaluate cloud spending patterns, giving recommendations and insights for optimization. They act as a bridge between finance, technology and business teams. They work with these teams to align cloud spending with business goals, educate teams on cost implications and participate actively in budgeting and forecasting processes. FinOps specialists use cloud cost management tools for automation and they also use tooling solutions to improve cost tracking, reporting and optimization efforts.

DevRel (for cloud platforms)

In the context of the cloud, someone working in developer relations (DevRel) for a cloud company serves as a link between the company and the developer community. A cloud DevRel professional focuses on fostering engagement, education and advocacy within the developer ecosystem. They play an important role in articulating the value of cloud technologies, demonstrating best practices and facilitating a vibrant community around the cloud platform.

A cloud DevRel's responsibilities often include speaking at conferences, workshops and online events to share insights into cloud technology and how to use it. They actively contribute to creating educational content such as tutorials, documentation and sample applications, aiming to empower developers with the knowledge needed to leverage the cloud effectively.

Building and nurturing communities is another crucial aspect of a cloud DevRel role. This involves creating spaces for developers to connect, share ideas and collaborate on projects related to the cloud platform. By also optimizing the product's developer experience, cloud DevRel professionals contribute to the overall success of the cloud company, ensuring that developers have the resources and support they need to thrive as they leverage the cloud platform.

A dynamic field

There are a lot more roles than this book can cover, and now that you've read about some of the typical roles in the cloud it's important to note that companies name job roles differently and sometimes the responsibilities associated with a specific role can vary. The field of cloud computing is dynamic and there is a diversity of roles with specialized focuses. Additionally, industry trends, organizational structures and specific business needs may influence the terminology used in job titles.

For instance, in different organizations, a role that involves managing cloud infrastructure can be called something different entirely, such as cloud engineer, cloud operations specialist, or cloud infrastructure architect. Similarly, a person in charge of optimizing cloud expenses may be referred to as a cloud cost analyst, FinOps engineer, or cloud financial specialist. The key is to thoroughly analyse job descriptions, criteria and responsibilities to understand each role's subtleties and how they connect with your skills and career objectives.

Furthermore, new positions that reflect emerging trends and challenges are coming up as the cloud evolves. As people solve more problems on the cloud and the industry continues to innovate, other job titles will emerge.

Cloud computing certifications and training

There are many certifications for cloud computing. And while you don't need to take all of them simultaneously, achieving a few that align with your goals where necessary can help you build your cloud portfolio and enhance your career prospects in the field. Here are some prominent cloud computing certifications and training programmes:

- *AWS Certified Solutions Architect – Associate:* This certification is offered by AWS and created for individuals who design distributed systems on the AWS platform. It covers various topics, including architectural best practices, security and cost optimization.
- *Microsoft Certified: Azure Solutions Architect Expert:* This certification from Microsoft focuses on designing solutions that run on Azure. It validates skills in virtual networks, storage and security and shows that the person has expertise in implementing solutions on the Azure platform.
- *Google Cloud Professional Cloud Architect:* This certification assesses the ability to design and plan cloud architectures on the GCP. It covers topics like infrastructure, data storage, security and more.
- *CompTIA Cloud+:* This global certification validates the skills needed to deploy and automate secure cloud environments that support the high availability of enterprise systems and data.

- *Certified Cloud Security Professional (CCSP):* This certification is offered by ISC2. It focuses on cloud security and is suitable for people responsible for ensuring the security of cloud environments. It covers topics like data protection, legal and compliance issues and risk management.
- *Certified Kubernetes Administrator (CKA):* This certification is sponsored by the Cloud Native Computing Foundation (CNCF). This programme aims to ensure that CKAs have the skills, knowledge and competency to perform the tasks of Kubernetes administrators.
- *Certified Kubernetes Application Developer (CKAD):* Also offered by CNCF, the CKAD exam certifies that people can design, build and deploy cloud-native applications for Kubernetes.
- *AWS Certified DevOps Engineer – Professional:* This certification from AWS is for professionals with expertise in DevOps. It validates continuous delivery, automation and monitoring skills on AWS.
- *Cisco Certified Network Associate (CCNA) – Cloud:* Cisco's CCNA – Cloud certification is designed for network administrators working with cloud technologies. It covers network fundamentals, network access, IP connectivity, IP services and security fundamentals.
- *Microsoft Certified: Azure Fundamentals (AZ-900):* This entry-level certification from Microsoft is designed for people who are new to Azure and cloud services. It covers fundamental concepts such as cloud concepts, Azure services, security and compliance.

Building a cloud computing career path

Embarking on a career in cloud computing may seem like a daunting task, especially when faced with the paradox of needing experience to secure a job but lacking the opportunity to gain that experience. But that does not mean it's impossible. In fact, there are several things you can do to support your entry into a cloud computing career, even if you don't have any prior experience.

First and foremost, learning new skills is super important. Websites like Coursera and Udemy have lots of classes on different cloud technologies. Take the time to understand the basics and get good at using the tools and platforms many companies use. Learning these skills helps build the proper foundation so that you feel more confident about what you know as you grow. Once you've learned the basics of cloud computing and you've taken some courses, you should prioritize getting hands-on experience.

Hands-on experience through internships is very important because you need a proven track record and work experience to be able to get better jobs as you grow. In the beginning of your career, actively look for internships at companies using cloud technologies. Internships let you dive into real projects, where you can apply what you've learned in the real world. They're like golden chances to boost your resume and get a deeper feel for how cloud computing works in practice.

Connecting with others is also super important. You cannot build your career alone; you need people. Networking helps you know what's happening in the industry and can plug you into referrals or other kinds of opportunities. Join in the cloud community – whether it's through forums, events, or professional networks like LinkedIn. Connecting with professionals already working in the field opens doors to mentorship, advice and even job opportunities.

It's also essential to approach your cloud computing journey with flexibility. Indeed, although there are a lot of times when you choose your career path, many times the career path chooses you. If you want to build a career in the cloud, don't be fixated on something like DevOps for example, because you might find out later that the company requires the skills you've built as a cloud software engineer or in the platform engineering department. Be open to exploring diverse roles within the domain, as your skills might find applications in unexpected areas. The industry is expansive and your adaptability will be a valuable asset as you navigate different opportunities. Career growth is not linear, and sometimes you might have to take unexpected turns to reach your desired destination, so being open-minded is crucial. Embrace the fact that your skills and experiences can lead you to exciting and unforeseen paths within the industry. Some professionals have successfully transitioned into the cloud from roles like backend engineering, showcasing the dynamic nature of career trajectories.

Remember, building a cloud career is not just about following a predefined route but also about creating your path based on evolving opportunities and your unique strengths. Don't be discouraged if your journey doesn't align with conventional expectations. Instead, view it as a chance to forge a distinctive, rewarding career in the cloud. Stay curious, keep upskilling, celebrate small victories along the way, learn from any setbacks, stay committed to your goal and be ready to adapt – eventually, with the right skills and access to mentorship and information, it will all make sense.

REVIEW

In this chapter, you learned about the different cloud computing job roles and some cloud computing certifications you can take as you start your career in the cloud. As you build your career in the cloud, embracing a growth mindset and prioritizing learning and networking are essential. Recognize that the cloud industry is dynamic, requiring continuous learning to stay relevant. Utilize educational platforms and certifications to upskill and actively network within the cloud community. By being proactive with your professional development, you position yourself for success as you build your cloud career. I wish you luck.

## CHAPTER THIRTEEN

Future trends in cloud computing

Previous chapters have discussed the different aspects and features of the cloud, from architecture to security, data, cost management, career navigation and even no-code tools. This is the current state of the cloud industry, but what about the future? In this chapter, we will review some of the future trends in cloud computing. As technology advances, the cloud is on the brink of significant changes. We will explore emerging trends that will shape the future of cloud computing.

Edge computing integrations

Edge computing is a distributed computing platform that brings enterprise applications closer to data sources like IoT devices or local edge servers. The major goal is to reduce latency and improve real-time processing by putting computational capacity closer to the source of the data. This proximity to data at its source results in major business benefits, such as faster insights, faster response times and optimal bandwidth utilization. The increasing demand for real-time processing and the necessity to overcome latency difficulties highlight the growing importance of edge computing.

Cloudflare is a company innovating at the network edge. Mainstream cloud providers like AWS and Azure are also starting to offer edge computing services. By offering edge computing capabilities, cloud providers empower businesses to optimize their workflows for real-time applications that require reduced latency and enhanced responsiveness. As the demand for edge computing continues to rise, we may see cloud providers expand and refine their offerings to meet the evolving needs of organizations that want to leverage the benefits of centralized and edge computing.

Advanced cyber security

As cloud usage grows, so do cyber security challenges. Because of the importance of protecting sensitive data and preserving the integrity of cloud environments, increasingly advanced cyber security measures are expected. Organizations and cloud service providers may invest even more in comprehensive security protocols, technologies and strategies to combat evolving cyber threats. This proactive strategy will protect cloud infrastructures from potential vulnerabilities, data breaches and unauthorized access as the cloud grows.

Sophisticated artificial intelligence

It's very clear that the cloud is an AI challenge. How and where do you train your models? Where do you store data? As we build more sophisticated AI solutions, cloud platforms will continue to enhance their capabilities. Cloud providers are becoming key players in addressing the complexities of AI by offering scalable infrastructure, computational resources and specialized tools tailored for efficient AI model training. The dynamic nature of the cloud enables organizations to access extensive computing power on demand, assisting in the training of increasingly complex and powerful AI models.

The cloud is a significant enabler for AI applications in the context of data storage. Cloud systems offer extensive and secure storage solutions for massive datasets required for training machine learning models. As AI solutions evolve, cloud providers' storage capabilities are likely to improve further in order to handle and give smooth access to the enormous amounts of data associated with AI applications.

Low/no-code platforms

In the coming years, we can anticipate the continuation of the trend that aims to make application development accessible to a broader audience. This is evident in the increasing popularity of no-code/low-code platforms. These platforms empower individuals who may not have a traditional development background to create applications without delving into complex coding processes. The overarching goal is to simplify the application development process and lower the barriers for entry, enabling a more diverse range of people to engage in and contribute to the creation of cloud-based applications.

Sustainability in cloud computing

Green cloud computing is a concept centred on utilizing technology in an environmentally responsible way. The emphasis is on using computers and other digital equipment in a smart and sustainable way to minimize adverse effects on the planet. In the continuous effort to protect the environment, future trends may include a focus on green cloud computing. This involves a greater reliance on renewable energy sources and initiatives aimed at reducing carbon footprints. A noteworthy example is Microsoft's commitment to sustainability through solutions like Microsoft Cloud for Sustainability, which integrates data to facilitate monitoring and management of environmental impact, showcasing a proactive approach toward eco-friendly practices.

Quantum computing

Quantum computers use quantum mechanical effects such as superposition and quantum interference to tackle certain tasks quicker than regular computers. This increased speed is especially useful in applications such as machine learning, optimization and physical system simulation. The introduction of quantum computing has the potential to revolutionize cloud computing capabilities. This can be seen by services such as Amazon Braket, a fully managed quantum computing service. Amazon Braket is designed primarily to expedite scientific research and software development in the field of quantum computing, demonstrating the integration of quantum capabilities into cloud services to drive creativity and problem-solving across multiple domains.

REVIEW

There will be improvements and future trends in addition to the few I've mentioned in this chapter, and it will be exciting to see the industry evolve and innovate further. Because of the fast-paced nature of the technology, it is conceivable that new breakthroughs and innovations will be revolutionary, stretching the boundaries of what we currently consider possible. Innovations in areas such as cyber security, networking (5G) and multicloud techniques have the potential to significantly alter how we view and interact with cloud computing.

Conclusion

Congratulations! You've successfully navigated through a comprehensive exploration of cloud computing, covering a wide range of important topics. This journey has equipped you with a solid understanding of cloud technologies, from diving into the details of cloud architecture, understanding the different cloud service providers and grasping the specifics of cloud storage to exploring big data analytics, virtual machines, containers and the details of cloud engineering.

You've set a solid basis for your cloud expertise by exploring platform engineering, discovering the potential of cloud no-code technologies and gaining insights into important topics like cloud security, migration strategies and cost management. The chapter on navigating cloud careers has provided significant insights into various positions and career paths within the cloud domain, while the study of future trends provides a view into the growing cloud computing world.

Completing this book is a significant achievement and I encourage you to reflect on the wealth of knowledge you've acquired. Remember that learning is an ongoing process and staying up to date with technologies is the key to continued success. Embrace a growth mindset, stay curious and adapt to the dynamic nature of the cloud industry. Whether you're embarking on a cloud career or expanding your existing expertise, the insights gained from this book will serve as a helpful guide. I wish you the very best in your endeavours as you move forward in your cloud career. I cannot wait to see what you build!

Index

NB: page numbers in *italic* indicate figures or tables

Looking for another book?

Explore our award-winning books from global business experts in Digital and Technology

Scan the code to browse

www.koganpage.com/digital-technology

Also in the Confident series

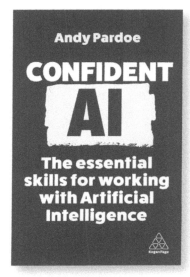

ISBN: 9781398615724

ISBN: 9781398616578

ISBN: 9781398611924

ISBN: 9781398611887

Printed in the USA
CPSIA information can be obtained
at www.ICGtesting.com
JSHW072047280624
65591JS00008B/62

9 781398 615670